ty TEACH YOURSELF

EXCEL 5

TEACH YOURSELF

EXCEL 5

Oxford Computer Training

Hodder & Stoughton

A MEMBER OF THE HODDER HEADLINE GROUP

British Library Cataloguing in Publication Data

ISBN 0 340 63947 4

First published 1995
Impression number   10 9 8 7 6 5 4 3 2
Year   1999 1998 1997 1996

Typeset by Oxford Computer Training.
Printed in Great Britain for Hodder & Stoughton Educational, a division of Hodder
Headline plc, 338 Euston Road, London NW1 3BH by Cox & Wyman Ltd, Reading,
Berkshire

List of Contributors

Ross Bentley, Jon Collins, Ian Cunningham, Shona McLeod, Andrew O'Connell, Gary Powell, Brian Reid, Julie Robertson, Narinderpal Singh Thethi, Pamela Stanworth, Donald Taylor, John Ward, Hugh Simpson-Wells, Wendy Tagg, Duncan Young.

—— CONTENTS ——

Acknowledgements

A number of products have been referred to in this book, many of which are registered trademarks. These are acknowledged as being the property of their owners.

The trademarks mentioned in this book include:

Microsoft: Windows, MS-DOS, Word for Windows 6, Excel 5, Access.

IBM: PC

Intel: i486, Pentium

1

— INTRODUCTION —

This chapter covers:
- The aims of this book.
- The conventions used in this book.

This book is intended for first time users of Microsoft Excel version 5. References to 'Excel' mean Microsoft Excel version 5. Occasionally, previous versions of the software will be mentioned in the text. References to these will include the version number explicitly.

This book aims to provide a basic understanding of the operation of Excel. It starts with some basic spreadsheet concepts, then goes on to show how simple but professional- looking spreadsheets and charts can be produced. It is assumed that you have a working knowledge of Microsoft Windows.

This book is not a definitive source of information, and should not be taken to be an authoritative document, merely a guide: an introduction to Excel and a supplement to its manual.

Conventions

Throughout this book, instructions that you must carry out are written

🖱 *like this (in italics, with a mouse graphic to the left).*

Anything that you must type is shown `in this style.`

Key words are shown like this: **DOS**, **button**, **Toolbar**, **mouse**.

Special keys are shown like this: Ctrl, T, etc. with combinations shown as Ctrl T (which means press T whilst holding down Ctrl).

On screen 'buttons' are shown like this: OK

Enter means the enter key (also known as carriage return, return, CR etc).

References to filenames are shown as `FILENAME.XLS`.

👍 *Hints and warnings about how to do things are often given in italics like this with a 'thumbs up' symbol at the start.*

🖝 *Text appearing in a box with this graphic is usually technical or an aside not strictly essential to the issue under discussion. You may prefer to skip it on the first reading.*

From time to time, you will see a box containing summary points which reinforce the section of text that they follow, like this:

Summary: Conventions in this book

- This book is for new users of Excel version 5 for Windows ('Excel'). It assumes a working knowledge of Windows.
- Instructions appear in *italics*. Text for you to type appears `in this style`.
- Keywords appear like this: **keyword.**
- This is a summary box, intended to reinforce the points made in the main body of the text.

2

BASIC PRINCIPLES

This chapter covers:
- The relationship between the computer, Windows, and Excel 5.
- Starting Excel.

What is Excel?

Excel is a spreadsheet program. It is used for manipulating numeric data in a grid of information. It can display this data in many ways, for example, as a table of information or as one of a variety of graphs. Because Excel operates in the Windows environment, it is a 'What You See Is What You Get' (WYSIWYG) package, showing your work largely as it will be printed – not only from the point of view of text attributes (bold, italics, typeface, etc.) and positioning – but also including pictures, tables and graphs.

———— What is Windows? ————

Microsoft Windows is a program that acts as a **user-interface** between you and your computer's Disk Operating System (DOS). With Windows applications a user can work with several programs simultaneously. It also provides an easy means of transferring information between applications. You could say that Windows provides services for applications like Excel and Word to use.

———— What is an application? ————

An application is a computer program designed to perform a particular task. Windows provides an operating environment under which a number of applications can run.

Windows comes with a number of standard applications. A variety of other Windows applications can be purchased, e.g. PowerPoint (presentation graphics); Excel, Lotus 1-2-3 (spreadsheets); Word, WordPerfect (word processors); Superbase, Access (databases). There are also many applications that are not specifically designed to run in the Windows environment. Such 'DOS' or 'non-Windows' applications can also be run from Windows, but may not be able to use all the services Windows provides.

Windows applications all make use of the Windows graphical environment in a standard way. This means that many of the skills and even everyday keystrokes are the same in most Windows applications. When you have learnt to use one Windows application you are already well on the way to mastering others. This approach is known as the Common User Interface (CUI).

Windows also allows you to load more than one application at the same time, and makes switching between them easy.

> ✍ *If you are using an 80386 or higher processor, you can even have several applications running at once.*

Starting Excel

If Excel is not installed on your computer, go to Appendix 2 for details of the installation process.

On your system, Excel may be started automatically. If this is the case, there is no need to start it again by any of the methods described below.

Starting from the Program Manager

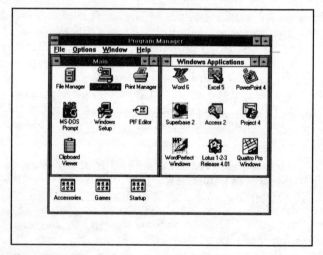

Typically, when Windows is started, the Program Manager will present a number of group windows, some open, some minimised as icons. One of these should include the Excel icon. If you can't see the Excel icon in any of the currently open group windows, try opening other groups (e.g. Accessories).

Excel can be started by double-clicking the Excel icon, or by clicking the icon and pressing [Enter]. If there is no Excel icon visible, you should be able to start Excel by choosing File Run and typing **EXCEL**.

Starting Excel directly

An application can be started (or **loaded**) directly from the DOS command line by typing the name of the program after the command to load Windows, e.g. **WIN EXCEL**. In such a case, the Program Manager will be loaded and minimised and Excel will be started.

Loading by Association

It is possible to start Excel from File Manager in two ways. One is to double-click the EXCEL.EXE filename. You can also start Excel by double-clicking an Excel file with an .XLS extension. This will also open the file you clicked as a Workbook.

Pre-loading Excel

It is possible to arrange for applications to be loaded automatically on starting Windows, either as icons or as windows.

Pre-loading an application is achieved by putting its icon in the StartUp group in Windows.

Summary: Methods for starting Excel

Excel can be started by using one of the following methods:

- Double-click the Excel icon in Program Manager.
- Type **WIN EXCEL** at the DOS prompt.
- Pre-load Excel by placing its icon in the StartUp group
- Use File Run from the Program Manager menu and type **EXCEL**.
- In File Manager, double-click a file ending .XLS.

3

THE EXCEL SCREEN

This chapter covers:

- Excel as it first appears when started.
- Standard Windows features: sizing buttons; the title bar; and control menus.
- The menu bar.

🖱 *Load Excel in the way that is appropriate to your system.*

If someone else installed your system then you should follow their specific instructions.

🖱 *Maximise the Excel window if it is not already maximised by clicking ▲ or double-clicking the window's title bar.*

A blank **workbook** is presented:

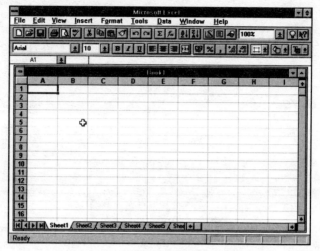

This workbook – Book1 – is displayed in a Window within the main Excel Window. You will find that you can move it around by dragging its title bar in the usual way but that you cannot move it outside the main Excel application window.

In order to see as much of the workbook as possible, you can maximise both the Excel application window and the workbook inside the window. You will do this shortly.

A workbook is one type of Excel **document** (others include Charts and Macro sheets). It is possible to have several document windows open at once in Excel, as with other Windows applications.

⎯⎯ Standard Windows features ⎯⎯

Title bars

If the document window is not maximised, two title bars are
visible. The application title bar (as above) gives the name of
the application (Microsoft Excel). The document title bar gives
the name of the document (Book1 in this case). Book1 is the
default name given to the document by Excel. Further workbooks opened during this session would be called Book2, Book3
and so on. When you save your work, Book1 will be replaced
with the filename you choose.

☟ *If it is not already maximised, maximise the document
window by clicking ▲ on its title bar.*

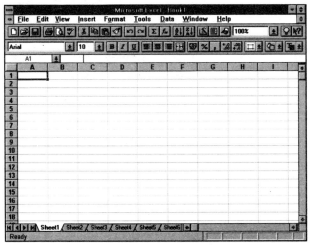

The document name now appears on the application title bar. If
you had several documents open, the currently active window

would be shown and its name displayed on the title bar. (The process of making different windows active is covered later.)

The menu bar

File	Edit	View	Insert	Format	Tools	Data	Window	Help

The menu bar is the horizontal strip immediately below the title bar. It has nine pull-down menus (File, Edit, etc.) in addition to the workbook window's control menu ▭ (when the workbook window is maximised). Many of the menu options are similar to those found in other Windows applications. In this book, you will probably be surprised to see how little use is made of the menus. Excel allows access to its most commonly used features in more convenient ways, such as buttons on the toolbar, or clicking the right mouse button to display shortcut menus.

Selecting a menu

Menus can be selected with the mouse, or by pressing ⌷Alt⌷, or F10) followed by the underlined letter of the menu.

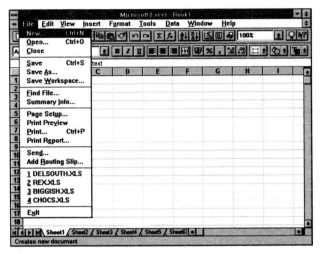

As an example, activate the File menu by clicking File (or by typing `Alt`, `F`).

A number of options are presented. Those that are not available appear in a different colour – typically grey – and may look dimmed. Notice that some menu options are followed by ellipses (...). These indicate that selecting such menu options will present the user with further options in the form of dialog boxes (see later).

This menu is similar to the File menu in many other Windows applications. Note that it includes the names of the last four files opened (if any) in Excel. These can be used for quick retrieval of your recent work (even after exiting and re-starting Excel).

A menu option may be selected by clicking it. When you do this, the option is chosen as you let go of the mouse button. There are, however, two alternative methods of making a selection. First, each menu has one letter underlined and that menu can be activated by holding `Alt` and pressing that letter. Each menu option also has an underlined letter. Once the menu is activated, typing this letter (with or without `Alt`), will select the option. Alternatively, once a menu has been activated, it is possible to select any option by using the cursor (arrow) keys to select a menu option, and then pressing `Enter`.

When an option is selected on the menu, a help message describing what the option does appears on the status bar at the bottom of the screen. This can be a useful way of reminding yourself what an option does. It can also be a useful way of browsing a menu to see what all the available options do. If you are dragging the mouse up and down a menu like this, and want to leave the menu without selecting anything, drag the mouse pointer off the menu and let go of the button.

Keyboard Shortcuts

Some of the menu options have keyboard shortcuts listed on the menu; e.g. Ctrl O for File Open... . This takes you to the File Open dialog – a menu of further options. The fact that a particular option does not have a keyboard shortcut listed next to it does not mean that a shortcut does not exist. There may be a shortcut that does more than simply taking you to the appropriate dialog. (For example, Ctrl Shift ~ applies Excel's default number format to the current selection; it is not on the Format menu as it applies a specific case of the Format Cells... dialog.)

Cancelling a menu

🖰 *To put a menu away, press Alt, or Esc twice, or re-click the menu title.*

👍 *The menus can also be cancelled by clicking anywhere that is outside the menu but this is not recommended. The click also has its 'normal' effect: selecting a cell, activating a button on a Toolbar, etc. Therefore, you may find that you make unintentional changes to your work as you are putting away the menus.*

Note: pressing Esc once will put away the menu but leave the menu bar active; in this case, a menu title will be left selected and you will be able to move the highlight across the menu using ← or →. The highlighted menu can be pulled down by pressing Enter. While a menu title is active, the keyboard cannot be used to enter data into cells; instead, the keys you press will select menu titles. To cancel a menu selection entirely, using Esc, you would have to press Esc a second time.

As you work with Excel, other menu options will become active as appropriate.

The mouse pointer

When working with Excel, the standard Windows mouse pointer ⍟ changes shape, depending on its position in the window. As an example: ⊕ appears in the worksheet area and is used to select cells; in the formula bar, you might see I , which is used to position the insertion point; you will also see ✚ in a later chapter; this is the AutoFill pointer.

The status bar

Ready		NUM	

The status bar is displayed at the bottom of the Excel window. Generally, it gives the message 'Ready', but it will also provide useful information about commands or toolbar buttons you are using.

> ☞ *The status bar can be switched off to make more space. If you haven't got a status bar, select Tools, Options. When the dialog box appears, select the View tab and check ☒ Status bar (i.e. click the status bar check box until it has a cross in it), then click* **OK** *. The status bar should now be visible. Similarly, the horizontal and vertical scroll bars may be turned on or off.*

────── The formula bar ──────

A1	↕ ☒ ✓ ƒ	

The formula bar appears just above the worksheet on the screen. When you select a cell, the formula bar will display its contents. The contents will either be figures, text or a formula that has been entered in that cell.

When you start entering data into a cell, ☒✓𝆑 appears on the formula bar, and the data you are entering appears next to this. ✓ and ☒ can be used either to accept or reject the changes made to cells.

To the left of the formula bar is the **name box**. The cell reference of the active cell (see later) will appear here. If a cell is **named**, the name will appear here. Naming cells is covered later.

Toolbars

Toolbars with push buttons appear (by default) just below the menu bar on the screen. There are several toolbars available and you will see shortly how to change which ones appear. By default, the **Standard** toolbar and the **Formatting** toolbar are displayed.

Toolbars provide a quick way of accessing common Excel commands. The Standard toolbar contains file handling and editing buttons (among others). The Formatting toolbar contains commands such as bold, italic and underline.

To illustrate the way toolbars give access to features try one. 🖼 is the button to Open an existing document.

Click 🖻

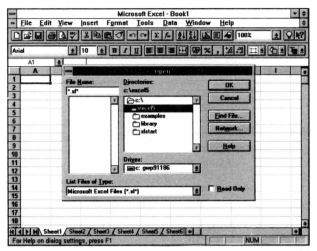

🖻 is a quick alternative to the File Open command.

 [Cancel] *the dialog and choose File Open.*

The same dialog was reached, this time by two clicks instead of one.

 [Cancel] *the dialog.*

Docking toolbars

Currently both toolbars are **docked** near the top of the screen. This means that they are displayed in a reserved area across the top of the workbook window. In this position they do not have a title bar and cannot be reshaped. However, the order that the toolbars are displayed in can be changed. Toolbars can also be docked at the sides or the bottom of the screen, or can be detached and allowed to float around the Excel window as 'mini-windows'.

Whether you work with your toolbars docked or undocked is a matter of preference. Undocking toolbars will give more space available for the worksheets. However, it may mean that you will want to move the toolbars when they obscure cells.

To move a toolbar, you drag it using the grey background of the toolbar; but you must take care not to click a button.

Undock the Formatting toolbar by dragging it down the screen until its outline changes shape, then let go of the mouse button.

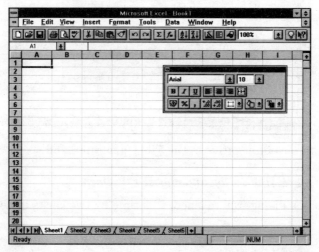

The toolbar is left floating in the middle of the screen In this state, it is referred to as being 'undocked'. Like any window, it has a title bar and can be re-sized.

To dock the toolbar at the edge of the screen, drag it to the edge of the screen until the outline of it changes shape to a long, thin rectangle. You can either use the toolbar's title bar or any part of the grey background of the toolbar to drag it.

🖰 *Use this method to dock the Formatting toolbar at the bottom of the screen.*

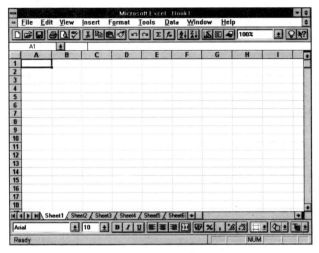

You can quickly re-dock or undock a toolbar by double-clicking a blank grey area of the toolbar. The toolbar jumps to its previous docked or undocked location (whichever it isn't in at the time).

🖰 *Double-click a blank area of the Formatting toolbar.*

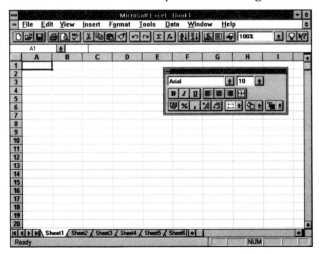

Removing and displaying toolbars

Excel has 13 toolbars as default. Different toolbars offer tools relevant to different kinds of Excel work. For example, you will see the Charting toolbar in a later chapter. It is not necessary (or desirable) to have all of the toolbars displayed at the same time, so Excel allows you to elect to show or hide the toolbars individually. There are two main ways of specifying which toolbars are displayed in Excel:

- By choosing the <u>V</u>iew <u>T</u>oolbars menu option; or
- By right-clicking any of the toolbars to display the toolbar shortcut menu.

It is also possible to hide an undocked toolbar by clicking its control box once.

Hide the Formatting toolbar by clicking its control box.

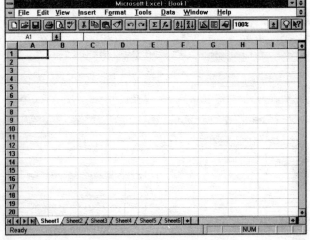

Displaying a toolbar

As an example, display the Microsoft toolbar. The tools on this toolbar will allow you to switch quickly between Microsoft packages installed on your computer.

·Choose <u>V</u>iew <u>T</u>oolbars.

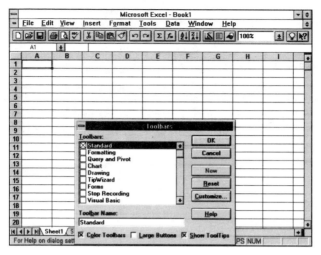

This dialog lists all the toolbars available. The checkboxes next to each indicate whether that toolbar is to be displayed.

🖑 *Scroll down the list, and check ⊠ Microsoft, then click* `OK`

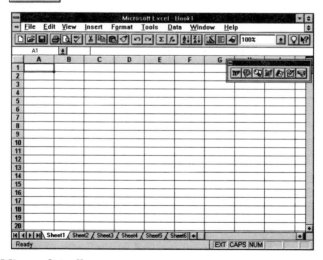

The Microsoft toolbar appears.

Hiding toolbars

🖱 *Right-click anywhere one of the toolbars.*

The toolbar shortcut menu offers a list of the nine most commonly used toolbars. A ✓ appears against those currently shown. The Toolbars dialog can also be reached through this menu. To either show or hide a toolbar, click its name in this menu.

🖱 *Choose the Microsoft toolbar from this menu to hide it again.*

Use either the Toolbars dialog or the shortcut menu to show the Formatting toolbar again, and relocate it at the top of the display.

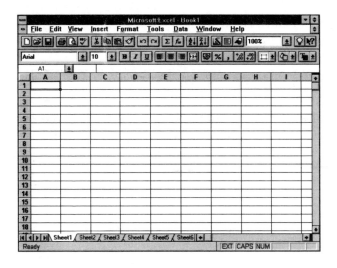

The workbook

The **workbook** is Excel's primary document. Each workbook is made up of a number of **worksheets** (the default number is 16). The worksheet 'Sheet1' is currently uppermost of the worksheets in 'Book1'. At the bottom of the worksheet are **tabs** relating to the first few worksheets in this workbook. The tab for Sheet1 is selected (it is the same colour as the worksheet itself), showing that Sheet1 is the 'active' worksheet. This means that any typing or commands will be applied to Sheet1. The tabs can be selected to switch between worksheets.

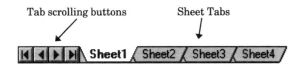

Click the tab for Sheet2.

This ability to work with multiple worksheets within a single workbook is an important feature of Excel 5. It will be covered in more detail in a later chapter. For now, it is important only to know that this feature exists, and to know how to switch between tabs (in case you do it accidentally).

 Click the tab for Sheet1.

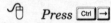

The Worksheet

Worksheets are composed of grids of **cells**. These are the boxes on the sheet at the meeting of columns and rows. Columns are labelled with letters; rows are labelled with numbers. For example, where column B and row 4 meet the cell is referred to as 'B4'. A worksheet contains 256 vertical columns and 16,384 horizontal rows, a total of over 4 million cells! This is the number of cells you *could* use, but it is unlikely you will ever actually need that many.

 Press Ctrl →

This takes you to the right-hand edge of the worksheet. Note that the last column is IV (256). The first 26 columns are labelled A to Z and then the 27th is labelled AA. The sequence continues AB, AC, ..., BA, BB, BC, and so on.

 Press Ctrl ↓

This takes you to the bottom row. The last cell on the worksheet is IV16384.

You can return quickly to cell A1 by pressing Ctrl Home

 Press Ctrl Home

You can also move around the worksheet using the scroll bars, located at the right and bottom edges of the display.

⌨ and ⌨ can be used to move the worksheet up or down one screenful. ⌨⌨ and ⌨⌨ will move the display left or right by one screenful.

 Experiment moving around the worksheet with the scroll bars and the keystrokes.

Summary: The Excel screen

- Excel exists within a main window, which will always have its own **title bar**.

- Each workbook can also have a window and title bar of its own. Often, the workbook window will be maximised; its title will then be appended to the Excel title bar.

- A **menu bar** appears under the Excel title bar. Excel menus are accessed from here.

- **Toolbars** give access to many of the most commonly used commands. They can be moved or hidden as is found convenient.

- The **status bar** shows various pieces of information, including brief help for commands on the menus.

- ⇧ is the most common pointer in Excel. It is used to select cells.

- Excel's primary document is the **Workbook**, which is made up of a collection of **Worksheets**.

4

WORKING
WITH CELLS

This chapter covers:

- Entering data in cells.
- Editing, moving and clearing cells.
- Right-click shortcut menus.
- The Undo feature.
- Using AutoFill.
- Simple formatting.

The cell and data entry

The cell is the basic unit of a spreadsheet. Information in the
spreadsheet is stored in cells. This information can either be
raw data such as names, titles or invoice figures, or formulae
which operate on the data. The cell can be formatted to display
the data or results of calculations in a number of ways. This
will be covered later in the chapter.

Cell references

As mentioned in Chapter 3, a cell can be identified by its unique column/row **cell reference** or **address**. A cell reference consists of the column letter followed by the row number, e.g. A1, A2, B3.

The active cell

This book will occasionally refer to a cell as the **active cell**. This means that the cell has been chosen as the 'target' for data you type in from the keyboard.

In the current worksheet, cell A1 should be the active cell. You can identify the active cell as it has a thick, lined border and its cell reference (or name, if it has one) appears on the left of the Formula bar. This area is known as the **name box**.

It is possible to select a block of cells or **range** and apply commands and options to the whole range (see later). The selected cells will appear reversed, apart from the active cell, which will retain the normal cell colour. All of these cells will be contained within a thickened **range boundary**.

The following diagram should help to clarify the terms used so far.

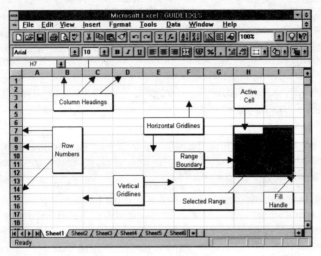

🖱 *Select cell A1 (using the cursor keys or by clicking the cell with the mouse).*

Type **text** *and then press* Enter

Type **45** Enter *in cell A2*

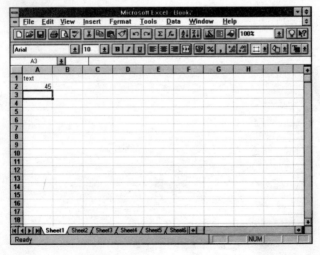

Text has been placed against the left edge of cell A1 on the worksheet, while **45** has been placed against the right edge of cell A2. When you pressed [Enter], Excel evaluated what you had typed as the contents of the cell. It treated **text** as text, and demonstrated this by displaying it to the left of cell A1 (the default way of displaying text). Excel treated **45** as a number, and demonstrated this by displaying it to the right of cell A2. This is how Excel treats these two types of data by default (this can be changed, as will be shown later).

Excel also moved the active cell down one row when [Enter] was pressed. This is default behaviour and can be modified so that the active cell does not move when [Enter] is pressed (by choosing an option on the Tools Options Edit dialog tab).

As well as entering data you can enter formulae. Excel will perform the calculations and (normally) display the results. Formulae are signified by typing = at the very beginning of the cell entry:

> *Make A3 the active cell by clicking it with the mouse or using the cursor (arrow) keys on the keyboard.*

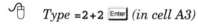 *Type =2+2 [Enter] (in cell A3)*

You should see:

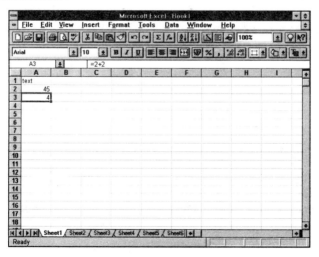

The result of the calculation **2+2** is shown in cell A3 on the worksheet display, but what you actually typed, **=2+2**, is still displayed in the Formula bar. This is how Excel works by default: in the Formula bar it displays what you actually entered; on the worksheet, it shows the result of its operations on the information.

With text or user-entered numbers, Excel displays what was typed. With a calculation, it performs the calculation and then displays the result on the worksheet. Note that Excel has placed the result of the calculation on the right of cell A3, indicating that it is treating the result as a number in its own right, and can perform calculations on that number.

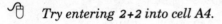   *Try entering 2+2 into cell A4.*

2+2 appears on the left of cell A4. Excel treats it as a piece of text because it was not preceded by =. You must use = to tell Excel that you are entering a formula.

More about data entry

So far, you have entered information cell by cell, treating each cell as a separate item. You can let Excel know that you want to fill in a table of cells by first selecting an area. Excel will then move the active cell from cell to cell automatically as you press Enter or Tab after entering the data for each cell.

Click the middle of cell A10 and hold down the mouse button.

Now drag the mouse pointer ✥ *across to cell B12 – note that Excel highlights all the cells in between as you drag.*

Finally, let go of the mouse button.

The thick border around the active cell has been extended to cover all the cells that you have selected. Those cells have all been highlighted, apart from the active cell. This mouse action has selected a cell **range**.

Having selected a range, you can easily enter data within it. You will find that you can move around this selected block using the [Tab] and [Enter] keys. Pressing [Tab] moves the active cell to the right, until you reach the right edge of the selection, whereupon the active cell 'wraps' to the leftmost cell on the next row down. At the bottom right of the block, pressing [Tab] makes the cell at the top left of the block become active. Holding down the [Shift] key while pressing [Tab] reverses the order of selection (first to the left and then up).

Pressing [Enter] moves the active cell down columns rather than along rows. Holding down [Shift] while pressing [Enter] reverses the direction.

Experiment with [Enter], [Shift][Enter], [Tab], and [Shift][Tab].

You can use these techniques to enter data into a selected block of cells without having to concentrate on keeping the right 'shape' for the block whilst typing. This can be especially useful in dealing with large tables.

Using the above techniques, enter the numbers 1 to 6 in the selected cells according to the pattern below.

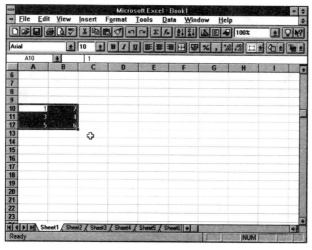

Be careful not to use the mouse buttons or cursor keys while entering the data as this will de-select the block and you will have to re-select cells A10 to B12.

Ctrl . moves the active cell clockwise to the next corner cell in the selection. This can be useful when working with large selections.

🖱 *Experiment with* Ctrl .

Cell editing

Often you will want to edit the contents of a cell, for example to correct a typing error or to change the information stored. Earlier it was shown that the Formula bar displays what was typed, while the worksheet display shows the result of that typing.

You can edit the contents of a cell using the Formula bar. To make the Formula bar active:

- Double-click the cell you want to edit; or
- Select the cell, then click the formula bar; or
- Select the cell, then press F2.

🖱 *Use one of these methods to edit cell A1.*

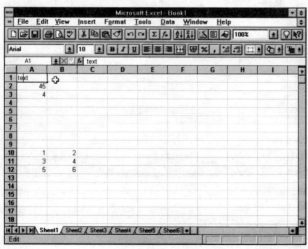

Excel is now in cell editing mode. The mouse pointer has changed to an I-beam shape (^{I}) to facilitate text editing. There is also a flashing vertical line, known as the insertion point (or cursor), somewhere in the middle of your text (its exact position will depend on which of the methods was used to activate cell editing mode). The insertion point can be moved through the text using the cursor keys or by clicking with the I-beam positioned at the desired point in the text.

> *Experiment with moving the insertion point within the cell using both of these methods.*

Text can be edited in this cell in the same way that it might be edited in a word processor. For example, ⌫ and Del delete text around the insertion point.

> *Change the text in cell A1 to read* **Here is some text.**

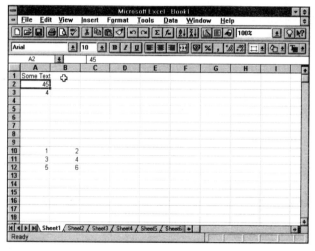

The text over-runs the width of the cell and (because the cell is left-justified) the text is displayed over the cell to the right. Excel allows text to be displayed in that space because the cell to the immediate right is empty.

Moving cells

Cells or blocks of cells can be moved around the worksheet by selecting them, 'picking them up' with the mouse and moving them somewhere else. This is known as **drag-and-drop**.

Before experimenting with this, it is useful to know the meaning of the different mouse pointers that might appear.

You will see that the mouse pointer changes shape depending on its position. When inside the active selection it appears as a large, white cross. Here, it can be used to select cells.

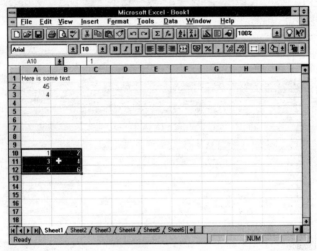

On the edge of the active selection it becomes a white arrow. This can be used to move or copy cells.

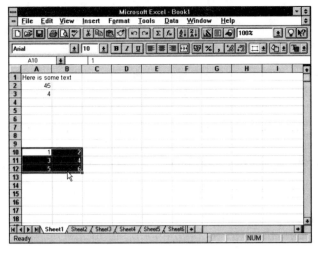

At the bottom right of the active selection it becomes a thin, black cross-hair:

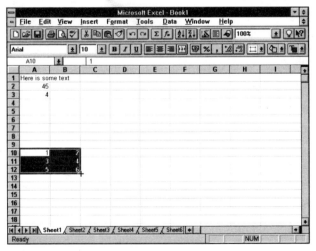

In this shape it is covering a small black square called the **Fill handle.** The function of the Fill handle will be covered later.

Make sure that you can see each of these.

To 'pick up' the selected block, the mouse pointer must be on the edge of the selected block (but not above the Fill handle at the bottom right) so that the white arrow pointer is showing.

🖱 *Position the mouse pointer over the middle of the bottom edge of the selected block of cells, with the white arrow pointer showing.*

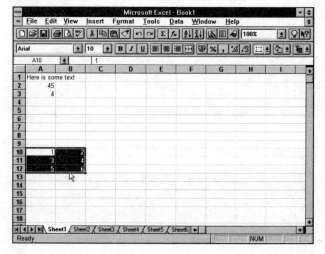

🖱 *Click and hold to pick up the block, then drag the grey outline until it surrounds cells G15 to H17 on the worksheet.*

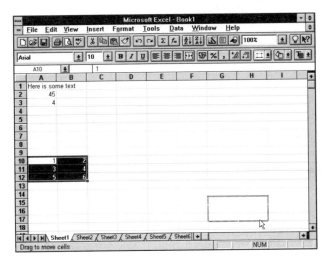

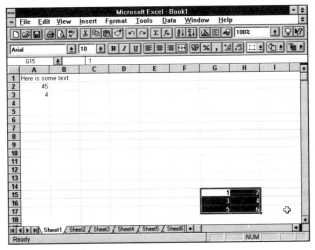

Now let go of the mouse button.

Dragging cells from one place to another causes them to be **moved**.

It is possible to force them to be **copied** by holding down Ctrl before letting go of the mouse button.

Select cells G15 to H17 and then drag the outline to cells A10 to B12, but do not let go of the mouse button yet.

Hold down Ctrl

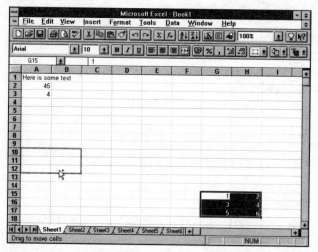

Notice that a small plus sign appears next to the arrow mouse pointer to indicate copying mode.

While still holding down Ctrl, *release the mouse button, then let go of* Ctrl.

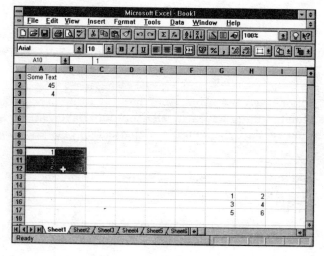

👍 *It isn't strictly necessary to hold down* ⌨Ctrl *throughout the whole operation – you need only be holding this key down when you release the mouse button for copying to occur.*

Clearing cells

You may want to remove the information in a cell, or cells. This operation is known as **clearing**. There are several ways of doing this.

🖰 *Select the block of cells G15 to H17.*

🖰 *Choose Edit Clear from the menu.*

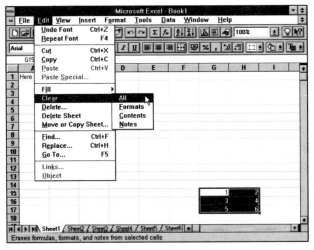

Four options are available from here, showing the different types of data stored for each cell. You may have noticed a De-lete option on the Edit menu. The distinction between clearing the cell contents and deleting the cell itself will be explained later. For now:

🖰 *Choose Contents.*

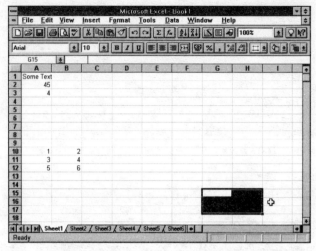

The cells are still present and selected, but their contents have been cleared. ⌫ is a useful keyboard shortcut for Edit Clear Contents: note that it does not Delete the cells, it merely Clears them.

The Undo command

Imagine that you had accidentally cleared the wrong cells, or simply changed your mind and decided you wanted the information back in the cells. Excel offers an Undo command which reverses the effect of the last command.

🖑 *Click ▨ (or select the Edit menu and choose Undo Clear).*

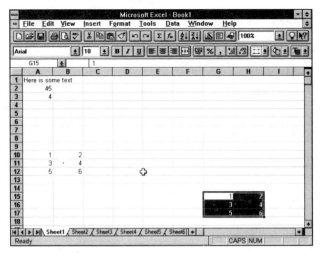

The Undo feature reverses the last operation, whether that was formatting, clearing, editing, etc. There is a keyboard shortcut, which is [Ctrl][Z]

☝ *There are some actions that cannot be undone, so you should be wary of relying on Undo.*

To complement Undo, there is a Redo command which allows you to redo whatever you have undone. Whenever you Undo something, the Undo option on the Edit menu will change to Redo.

Shortcut menus in cells

🖱 *Position the mouse over any of the cells in the selected block and click the right mouse button.*

The shortcut menu appears:

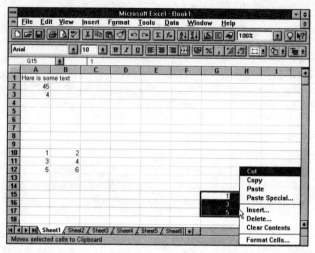

The options are drawn from various menus on the menu bar, e.g. Cut and Copy are identical to the Cut and Copy options on the Edit menu, whereas Format Cells relates to the Cells option on the Format menu. The Shortcut menus are often convenient, particularly as the options change according to the item which was right-clicked.

In this case, choose the Clear Contents option.

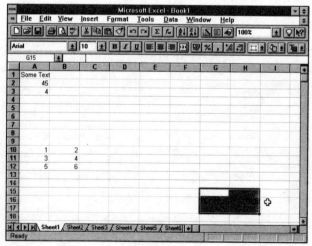

This has once again removed the numbers from the selection, and is equivalent to Edit Clear Contents or Del

You should now be familiar with the idea of alternative methods for achieving the same end. None of the methods is more 'correct' than another (although some may be quicker or slower). It is up to the individual to decide which method or methods they prefer. For the moment, it is important to realise that choices of equal merit exist, and that you can use any combination of methods that suits you.

AutoFill

AutoFill is used to extend series of data automatically, removing the task of typing in every item in what might be a long series. It is this operation which uses the Fill handle at the bottom right of the active cell, or block of cells.

The use of the Fill handle will be covered using dates as an example, but can be applied to almost any sequence of data. For example, you might want to type in the first six months of the year in a row of 6 cells.

Type Jan into cell A13, press Enter *and then make A13 active by clicking it.*

Position the mouse pointer over the bottom right corner of cell A13, so that the ⊕ pointer changes to a black cross-hair (✚) – indicating that you have correctly located the mouse over the Fill handle.

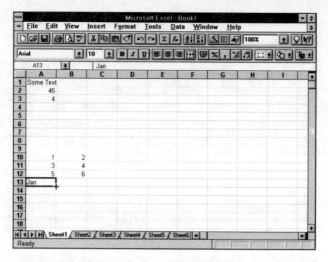

🖱 *Drag across to cell F13.*

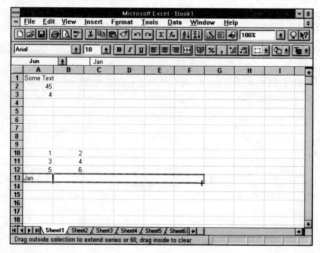

Now release the mouse button.

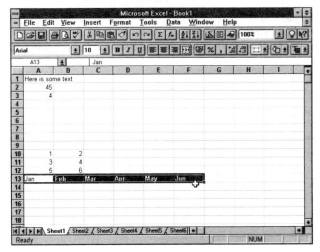

Excel has various common series built-in: it knows that 'Jan' is a month, and what the rest of the series is.

You could use AutoFill to enter a series of consecutive numbers.

Type 20 into cell A14 and 21 into cell B14. Select the cells, then position the mouse pointer over the Fill handle.

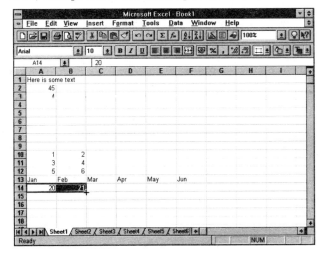

Drag to fill the series across to cell F14.

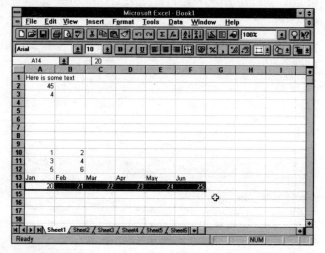

Excel AutoFills the selected cells with an increment of +1 from cell to cell. This is an extremely powerful feature of Excel. It will be covered in more detail in the section on formulae in Chapter 5 and again in Chapter 13

——— Basic formatting ———

So far, Excel has chosen the formatting of cells. However, you can choose different formats. For example, the typeface and colour of characters can be changed and they can be displayed as bold, italic or underlined. Many of the common formatting commands can be found on the Formatting toolbar. If you can't immediately see which icon does what, you can use ToolTips – just let the mouse pointer hover over a tool for a second or so, and a ToolTip should appear letting you know what it does.

> *If this doesn't work, it may be that the feature has been turned off; if you want to turn it on again, take the Toolbars option from the View menu and make sure ⊠ Show ToolTips is checked.*

🖰 *With cells A14 to F14 still selected (the 'month' cells) you might like to alter them to be right aligned –* ▣▣▣ *respectively format left, centre and right.*

🖰 *Select cell A1, and experiment to try and find out which ones control text appearance.*

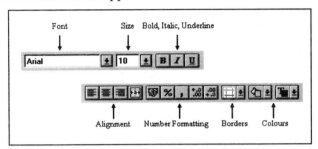

🖰 *You might like to use these buttons to format the text in cell A1 to be Times New Roman Italicised 14pt:*

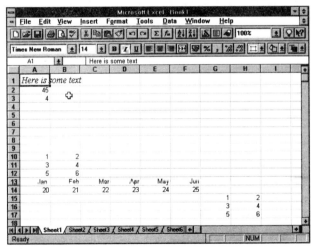

Formatting will be covered more fully in a later chapter.

Part of the text in cell A1 appears to be in cell B1. In fact, all the text is still stored in cell A1, but as the text is too long to fit into the display of cell A1, Excel allows the blank cell B1 to have its display overwritten.

If there had been anything in B1, the overwriting would not have occurred and you would only be able to see the amount of text that Excel could fit into the cell A1 display. Under these circumstances you might want to increase the width of the column. This is certainly possible, but there is a special feature – 'Best Fit' – which re-sizes a column so as to accommodate the widest data in the column – useful if the column is too long to see on the screen at once.

Position your mouse pointer in the grey row of column headings and on the dividing line between columns A and B. A new mouse pointer ✛ appears.

With ✛ displayed, double-click.

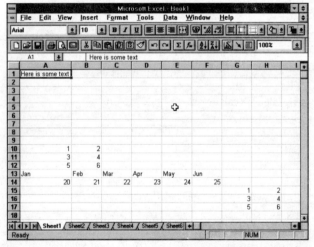

Column A has been re-sized to accommodate the text which occupies the greatest width. You could also drag the column with ✛ to make it wider, but double-clicking prompts Excel to 'best-fit' the column, based on the widest cell contents in the column.

Clearing Formats

If you have added a lot of formatting to a cell and wish to re-move it, you can clear any formatting for a cell (or cells) using Clear from the Edit menu and then choosing the Formats sub-menu.

While you are experimenting, you may find some unexpected effects owing to cell formatting. As well as text being formatted, numbers (and dates – see later) can be formatted, e.g. £3 in-stead of 3.00 (or 1/Jan/96 instead of 1/1/1996). If you enter a number (or date) in a particular form (say £3), then overtype it with something quite different (4.12), Excel may try and dis-play it using the same format (£4). Formatting is covered in full later on, but at least you know how to clear the format, and start again!

Summary: Working with cells

- The active cell can be edited either by double-clicking or by pressing [F2]
- Several cells can be selected with the ✛ pointer.
- Cells can be moved by dragging the range boundary with ↖.
- The Fill handle ✛ can be used to fill a range of cells rapidly with a series of numbers or text.
- Cells are cleared most simply by pressing ⊟
- ↶ is the Undo tool, undoing the last operation. [Ctrl][Z] is the keyboard shortcut for this.
- The Formatting toolbar provides many buttons that help you format the worksheet.
- Any formatting for a cell can be cleared via the Clear option on the Edit menu.

5

—— FORMULAE ——

This chapter covers:
- How to create a simple spreadsheet.
- Building up a table of calculations.
- Devising basic formulae.
- Making further use of the Fill handle.

—— Setting up a basic spreadsheet ——

Creating a new workbook

When setting up a new spreadsheet, you will probably want to start with a blank 'page'. You can do this either by selecting an unused sheet in the current workbook, or by creating a new workbook. Since this new spreadsheet will be unrelated to the spreadsheets you have done so far, it makes more sense to start a new workbook.

This can be done:

- By choosing File, New
- Using the new workbook tool,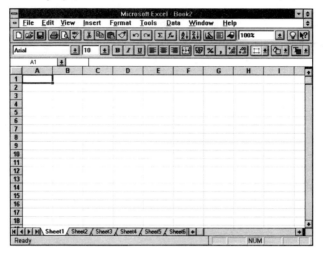
- By pressing Ctrl N

☞ *Use any of these methods to create a new workbook.*

Entering the data

In this example, you will set up a spreadsheet showing the stock data for Charlie's Confectionery Shop. The spreadsheet will record information about current stock levels and prices, and use this to calculate the value of the stock.

The sheet will need a title to describe what it is about.

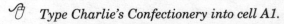 *Type Charlie's Confectionery into cell A1.*

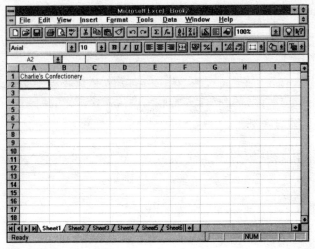

The basis of the table will be the nett price per pound (price/lb) of Charlie's sweets:

Item	Price/lb
Gobstoppers	1.12
Jelly Babies	1.09
Nut Brittle	0.85
Fruit Gums	1.2
Sherbert Dips	1.45

🖰 *Enter the information in cells A3:B8 (as shown in the table above) either using the range selection technique you saw earlier, or by selecting each cell in turn:*

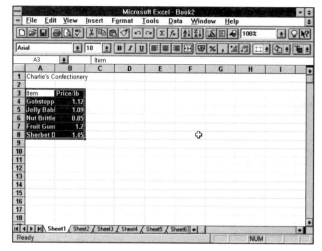

You should find that whether you type 1.2 or 1.20, the price of Fruit Gums remains stubbornly at 1.2. The appearance of numbers is a formatting issue, and is explained fully in the 'More Formatting' chapter – it makes no difference mathematically.

You should also find that the names in column A have been truncated. The reason is that the column is not wide enough to show all of the information. Don't worry about this just yet.

Devising and entering formulae

Having entered the prices, it is possible to perform calculations involving them, such as working out the VAT (Value Added Tax). This tax is currently 17.5% in Britain, so column C will contain 17.5% of the prices shown in column B. Excel will calculate these amounts for you.

First, enter a column heading for the VAT:

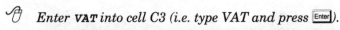 *Enter* **VAT** *into cell C3 (i.e. type VAT and press* Enter *).*

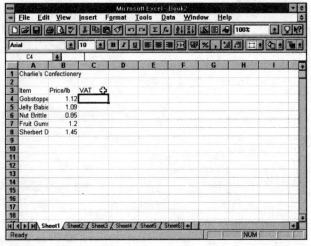

You will enter a **formula** to calculate the VAT into the cells in column C.

As you saw in an earlier section, formulae begin with =. This is a signal to Excel that the expression which follows must be evaluated. Consider cell C4: the value in this cell will be 17.5% of £1.12. However, since the (nett) price per pound of gobstoppers may change, the formula entered will refer to cell B4 itself, rather than to the current value in that cell.

Typing =**B4** into cell C4 would display the value of B4 in the cell. The content of C4 is not the value that is held in B4, but the formula that refers to it. The ability to make cells refer to the values of other cells rather than containing the values themselves is an important property of spreadsheets. If, later on, the contents of a cell referred to in a formula changes, the cell containing that formula can recalculate to reflect the new value.

So the formula =**B4*****17.5%** will calculate VAT on the value of B4.

 You may be unaware that the multiplication symbol used in computer environments is * (an asterisk) – this avoids the danger of mistaking a cell reference (like x24) for 'multiply by 24'. Division is indicated by / (a forward slash).

 Select cell C4

 Type =

 Click the cell holding the price of the gobstoppers

This is actually cell B4, but you don't need to know this – just click it.

 Type ***17.5%**

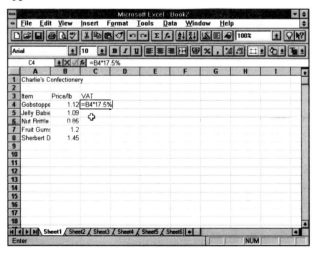

 Press Enter

The answer will be displayed (though if you select cell C4 again, the formula bar will remind you of the contents (the formula).

👍 *Notice that while you could have typed the reference to B4, we suggested that you clicked it. Using this 'point and click' method, you clearly indicated the data to be used in the calculation, without the danger of a typing error.*

✍ *Normally, you would not put a constant (such as the VAT rate) in a formula in this way. If the rate of VAT changes, the formula would have to be updated each time. There is a more efficient method which achieves the same result as the above example. This is covered at the end of the chapter.*

Copying formulae with the Fill handle

The remaining four cells in this column each require a formula. The formula will be slightly different in each case, as it will refer to a different cell in the column.

In this case, typing the formulae for each of the other cells in the column wouldn't take long, but imagine if there were hundreds of prices!

To cope with this situation, Excel provides a tool for copying formulae – the Fill handle. You used this earlier to create the list of the months of the year). It can also be used to copy formulae to other cells in a column or row.

Select cell C4, then use the Fill handle to AutoFill the formula down into cells C5:C8.

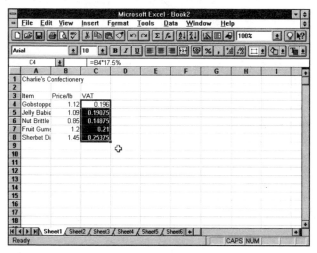

Select each of the cells C5:C8 in turn and look at what is displayed in the formula bar.

AutoFill has adjusted the cell references so that they refer to the equivalent cell for each row – for instance, VAT on Fruit Gums is given by `=B7*17.5%`.

The next column will list the prices including VAT – the gross prices.

Enter **Gross Price** *into cell D3.*

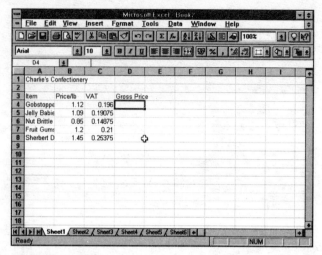

The calculation in this column will be 'Price/lb + VAT'. Therefore, for cell D4, the formula will be **=B4+C4**

Enter the formula into cell D4.

Again, we suggest you use 'point and click' wherever you can: press ⌐, click the price of gobstoppers, press ⌐, click the VAT for gobstoppers and press Enter

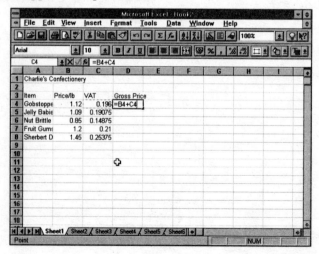

Again, the Fill handle can be used to complete the rest of the column:

 Use the Fill handle to copy the formula to cells D5 to D8.

	A	B	C	D	E	F	G	H	I
1	Charlie's Confectionery								
2									
3	Item	Price/lb	VAT	Gross Price					
4	Gobstoppe	1.12	0.196	1.12					
5	Jelly Babie	1.09	0.19075	1.09					
6	Nut Brittle	0.35	0.14875	0.85					
7	Fruit Gums	1.2	0.21	1.2					
8	Sherbet Di	1.45	0.25375	1.45					

Microsoft Excel - Book2 — File Edit View Insert Format Tools Data Window Help — D4 =B4+F8

You may think that the numbers in this table look a bit messy at the moment, but don't worry about this for now.

Naming cells

So far you have seen that it is possible to refer to a cell using the column and row headings. It is also possible to give a cell or a range of cells a **name**. This can be used to identify the cell or cells instead of using the cell reference.

There are several advantages in using names instead of standard referencing (e.g. A1, B1):

• Names are easier to remember than cell references since they can be specific to the spreadsheet and task that you are working on.

• Names make it much easier to read worksheets.

• Names make it easier to change the structure of the sheet.

• Named ranges can be referred to from other sheets.

- It is easy to Go To a named range or cell (using [F5]).
- Names used in formulae are not adjusted during a copy, whereas references are. This the particular advantage of names in your example.

First let's discuss the problem; then we'll try a solution that doesn't work; then we'll use a name.

✐ *Select cell C4*

Consider this cell. The current formula is `=B4*17.5%`. In future, there may be changes in the rate of VAT. To make more efficient use of the spreadsheet, it may be worth entering the rate of VAT in a suitable cell (just once). Then, instead of putting the rate itself (17.5%) in the formula in cell C4 (for instance) it would then be possible to refer to the cell containing this rate.

Should the rate of VAT change at a later date, only one cell would have to be changed, rather than having to check the entire spreadsheet (which could be large and complex) for entries of 17.5% (or whatever).

✐ *Select cell G1 and type* `VAT Rate`. *Select H1 and type* `17.5%`.

It is now possible to refer to cell H1 instead of typing the rate of VAT into a formula. Of course this means replacing your existing calculations, so you may as well clear them.

Select cells C4 through to C8 and clear them, either via the Edit menu or by pressing ⌫.

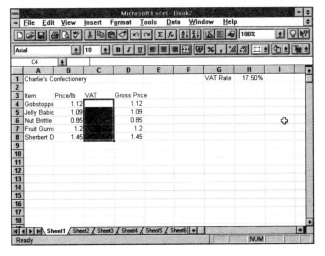

Enter the new formula =B4*H1

You can leave the whole range of cells selected if you like. Again, you can use 'point and click', typing only the operators (= and *).

Use the Fill handle to copy the formula to the other cells.

The result is something of a disappointment!

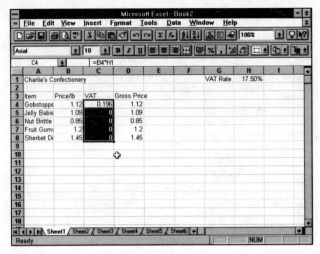

It is very important to understand why this hasn't worked. If you examine the formulae in the successive cells of the range, you will see this:

Cell	Formula	Comment
C4	=B4*H1	What you entered
C5	=B5*H2	Adjusted for the next row down
C6	=B6*H3	And so on
C7	=B7*H4	
C8	=B8*H5	

B4 has been adjusted, quite correctly, to B5, B6 etc. But H1 has also been adjusted (to H2, H3 etc.), which is not what you want. This 'problem' can be overcome using **absolute cell references** which we do not cover in this introductory book. Instead you are going to use named ranges – a simpler, and in many cases, a more satisfactory method.

Defining a name

🖑 *Select cell H1, click the drop-down (▼) beside the Name box in the formula bar and type in* **VAT**

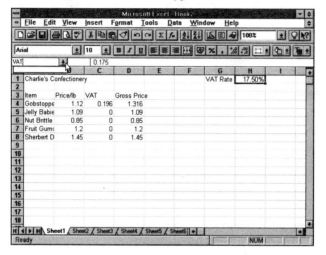

🖑 *Press* Enter

The name box no longer displays the cell reference. You should now see VAT in the box. You can now refer to 'VAT' whenever you wish to refer to that cell.

🖑 *Select cell C4 and look at the formula.*

The name has not been applied to the formula yet. To do this:

🖑 *Edit cell C4 (double-click or press* F2 *).*

🖑 *Delete the reference H1, and replace it with* **VAT**

🖑 *The formula should now be B4*VAT.*

🖑 *Press* Enter *to complete the edit, and use the Fill handle to copy the formula to the other cells.*

The result appears as before:

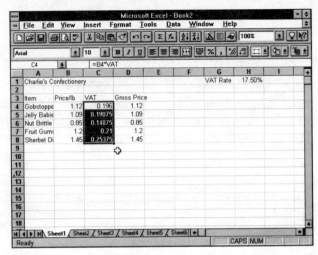

But this is a much more flexible spreadsheet model than it used to be. If the tax rate changes, you make one edit and your entire spreadsheet reflects the new rate.

 Change the rate to 12.50% (wishful thinking!):

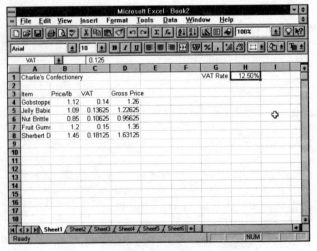

🖱 *Change it back again using 🔄 or* `Ctrl` `Z`

👍 *Use names for 'constants' like tax rates whenever you can – it saves you work in the long run.*

———— Order of calculation ————

When Excel calculates a formula it does not work from left to right (as many simple pocket calculators do); it uses a precedence system (which most 'scientific' calculators do). School children are often taught the acronym 'BODMAS' for remembering this system. This stands for Brackets Off, Division, Multiplication, Addition and Subtraction, which indicates the order in which the operations calculated. A few example should help:

6–4 * 5 = 10	according to a simple calculator
6–4 * 5 = -14	according to Excel (using 'BODMAS')
(6–4) / (8–7) = 2	again using 'BODMAS'

You might like to experiment, so that you feel confident with formulae.

———— Saving as you go ————

If you switch off the machine before saving this workbook, or for some reason Excel crashes before you have saved your worksheet, you will lose your work. The workbook on screen is only in the computer's 'RAM' (i.e. its non-permanent memory) This will be forgotten by the computer if it is switched off before the information has been saved onto a disk, which can store information after the power is switched off.

🖰 *Click* 🖫

Once a workbook has been named and saved, clicking 🖫 will save it again. This workbook has not been named, so the Save As dialog is presented.

Save As

You are prompted to choose a suitable drive and directory, and to give the workbook a name, 'book2' (or similar) is suggested:

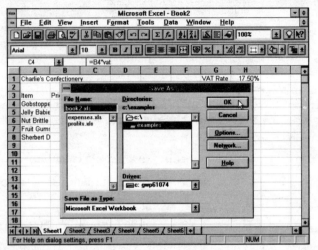

You can use the list boxes to navigate around the drives and directories to choose the most appropriate place for the file to be stored. After the document has been saved, you should be returned to your presentation, ready for more editing.

✒ *Save your presentation as* CHARLIE.XLS *by typing* **CHARLIE**

(The .XLS will be added automatically if you just call it CHARLIE).

Summary Info

Depending on how Excel is configured (whether or not you have ☒ Prompt for Summary Info checked on the General tab of the Tools Options dialog), you may be presented with the Summary Info dialog. Here you should fill in as much as you find useful; the fields are discretionary, offering you an opportunity to record data about the workbook file which might help with locating and identifying this workbook at a later date (see **Chapter 8**).

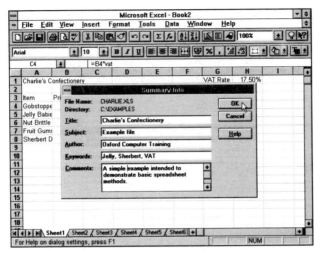

🖐 *Fill in suitable data in the Summary Info dialog, as we have done in the screenshot above, using* 〔Tab〕 *or the mouse to move between text boxes.*

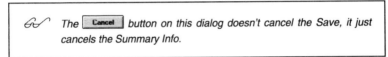

☞ *The* 〔Cancel〕 *button on this dialog doesn't cancel the Save, it just cancels the Summary Info.*

👍 *As already mentioned, if the workbook already has a name, when* 🔲 *is clicked, the latest version of the work is saved with that name and at that location, overwriting the earlier version. It is good practice to save frequently in this way, just in case of a power break or unexpected computer crash.*

Summary: Formulae

- All formulae are entered beginning with =.
- The value of another cell can be used by entering the other cell's reference (e.g. B4, C16, etc.). In this way, the formula can be recalculated after any change in the values of the cells to which it refers.
- A formula can be copied using the Fill handle. This will adjust the formulae in the destination cells so that they refer to equivalent cells.
- A cell can be named. This name can then be used in formulae. Names in formulae are not adjusted during copying.
- Excel does not calculate formulae on a left to right basis but uses 'BODMAS'.
- It is wise to save regularly using 🖫. If the workbook does not yet have a name, the Save As dialog will appear (this can always be invoked through the Save As... option on the File menu).

6

──── FUNCTIONS ────

This chapter covers:
- Different ways of entering Functions.
- The AutoSum tool.
- The Function Wizard.
- Some arithmetical functions.

──── The purpose of a function ────

Functions form the 'engine' of your spreadsheets. They allow you to include the result of possibly very complex calculations in your formulae without the need for you to understand or develop the underlying mathematics. There are over 450 different functions available in Excel, each one designed to perform a specific task. They range from relatively simple functions such as adding numbers, to complex calculations involving regression analysis, matrix manipulation or complex numbers.

Functions provide simple access to the calculating power of Excel. For example: suppose you wished to calculate the average of some numbers in a range. You could write instructions for this to a number of levels of detail:

Most detailed level:

1. Choose a cell in which to put your running calculation (a 'temporary storage' cell).

2. Choose another cell in which to keep a count of how many items are to be averaged (a 'counter' cell – initially 0).

3. Select the top left of the range of cells to be averaged.

4. Get the number in the current cell (if there is no number assume 0).

5. Add the number to the 'temporary storage' cell.

6. Add one to the counter cell .

7. Look for the next cell in the range.

8. If there are no more cells divide the temporary storage by the count and stop (possibly clearing your temporary cells); otherwise select the next cell (just identified).

9. Go to point 4 (and carry on).

Next Level:

1. Add the numbers in the range.

2. Count the numbers in the range.

3. Divide the total arrived at in point 1 by the total arrived at in point 2.

Highest Level:

1. Find the average of the numbers.

The Lowest Level is very tedious. Constructing even moderately complex spreadsheets in this way would be unrealistic. The middle level is manageable, but the highest level is clearly the most appropriate. Functions work at this level.

However sophisticated Excel might be, it still needs to be given certain pieces of information in order to perform as desired. Imagine that you wanted someone to buy a pint of milk for you. If you just said 'go and buy', you would not be very surprised if the person either asked for more information or came back with something entirely different. On the other hand, the instruction 'Go to the corner shop and buy a pint of milk, please' should give any reasonably intelligent person enough information to do exactly as you want.

Similarly, you cannot give Excel the instruction AVERAGE and expect it to average the correct numbers. You must elaborate on the instruction by telling Excel which numbers are to be averaged. These extra pieces of information are known as **arguments** to the function.

Actually, as you will see shortly, Excel will sometimes guess the right list of numbers when summing, but this is a very special case.

Functions are written in the form:

`=function(item1,item2,item3…)`

———————— Using a function ————————

Suppose that you wish to work out an average of the (nett) price per pound of your items, in cell B9.

The AVERAGE() function will do this. It averages a list of numbers, so `=AVERAGE(B4,B5,B6,B7,B8)` would do the job. However, although this formula is valid, the construction would become tedious for larger lists of numbers, and would require editing each time the length of the list was altered (e.g. by inserting or deleting rows of data).

Ranges

One extremely useful facility Excel provides with functions is that the arguments do not have to be single cell references: they can be numbers, other formulae/functions, or they can be range references. A **range** is a rectangular block of cells (a partial row or column, or a two-dimensional range). The set of cells from B4 to B8 is a range, which can be represented as B4:B8 (it can just as easily be represented as B8:B4). A simple range is represented by two cell references separated by a colon.

The two cell references represent opposite corners of the range, e.g. A1:C3 represents cells A1, A2, A3, B1, B2, B3, C1, C2, C3 (A3:C1, A3:C1 and C3:A1 will also work).

This means that the function for the example can be written =AVERAGE(B4:B8). Not only is this a much quicker way of writing the function (particularly for very large ranges), but the range can be easily extended to include other cells, as you will see later.

Even better, a point and click method can be used for indicating the range – simply click one corner of the range, and drag with the mouse to the opposite corner. This cuts down on errors, and means that you don't even have to think what the cell references are.

✍ *Select cell B9 and type* =**AVERAGE(**

It doesn't matter whether this is typed in UPPER-CASE or lower-case characters.

Drag so as to select cells B4 through to B8.

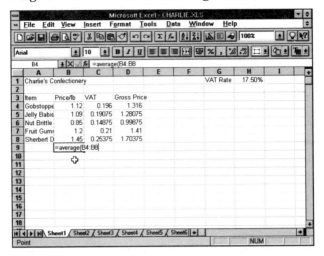

 Type) *and press* Enter

You have your average.

The SUM function

Perhaps the most important, or at least the most used, function is **SUM()**. This is used for summing (totalling) partial rows and columns, or any range or other selection of cells.

There is little purpose in calculating the total of the Price/lb, VAT or Gross Price (they would not be very meaningful), but with the addition of some extra information you can provide some good examples of function use.

You will add a new column to record the stock level of each product, and eventually a further column to hold the total gross retail value of stock (derived from the gross price and the stock level). It might be desirable to sum either of these columns – and that is what you'll do.

✍ *Enter the information for the stock level (in lbs), as shown below in cells E3 to E8:*

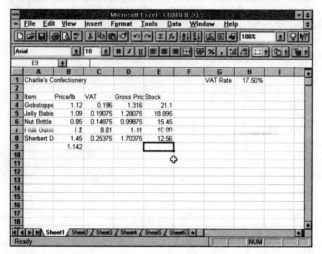

✍ *Select cell E9, if it is not already selected.*

The formula `=E4+E5+E6+E7+E8` would sum the contents of the stock column. The sum could also be performed by typing `=SUM(E4,E5,E6,E7,E8)` or `=SUM(E4+E5+E6+E7+E8)`. As in the AVERAGE() example the use of a range is more flexible.

As you have already seen in the case of AVERAGE(), you can use a range here: =SUM(E4:E8)

Remember, not only is this a much quicker way of writing the function (particularly for very large ranges), but the range can be easily extended to include other items and there is the added bonus of using point and click to enter the range, helping to avoid mistakes.

The AutoSum tool

You could type the formula `=SUM(E4:E8)`, perhaps using the mouse to drag the range reference, but because SUM is (probably) the most commonly used function, Excel provides a toolbar button for it: the AutoSum tool , which is normally found on the Standard toolbar:

🖱 *Click on the Standard toolbar.*

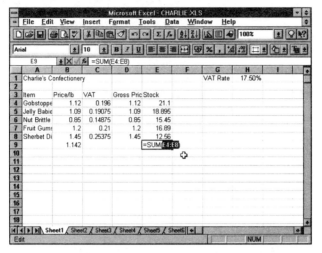

AutoSum tries to find a range to sum, following fairly simple rules. In this case, it has selected the correct range. AutoSum will always suggest the set of numbers in the partial column directly above or the partial row to the left of the selected cell (choosing the closest range if there are two nearby, and choosing the partial column above if there are two equally close).

If you want a range other than that which AutoSum suggested, select the range you want by dragging with the mouse.

🖱 *Click* Σ *again (or press* Enter *) to enter the sum.*

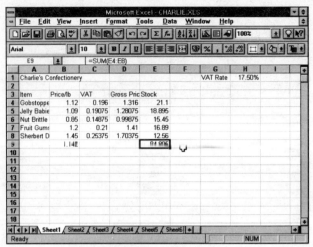

The result of the sum will appear in the cell that was selected when you invoked AutoSum.

Perhaps you'd like to use column F to show the nett retail value of the stock Charlie is keeping. This will be the nett price price/lb of the stock multiplied by the amount of stock.

🖱 *Type* **Retail Value** *into cell F3.*

🖱 *Enter the appropriate formula into cell F4:* **=E4*B4**

👍 *Remember that you can click the stock level of Gobstoppers (B4), type the '*' and click the price of Gobstoppers (E4) – without actually thinking in terms of cell references.*

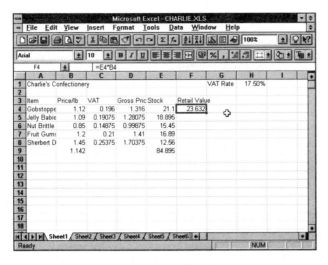

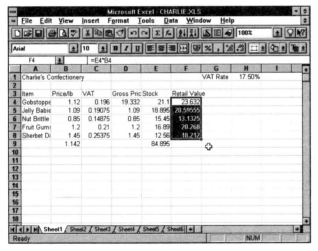

Use the Fill handle to copy the formula into cells F5:F8

F9 can be used to display the total value of stock.

Select cell F9.

From the rules given above, you can predict that AutoSum will suggest the cells you want totalled in F9. Clicking the tool twice will put the total in the selected cell more quickly (since you are confident that AutoSum will 'guess' right).

☞ *Click* ⊠ *twice to enter the function.*

When to use SUM

It is important to realise that SUM() is just another function. The AutoSum tool (⊠) is provided because it is so popular, but if you were to get involved with the more advanced features of Excel, you would soon learn that an AVERAGE button could be provided too.

=SUM() should be used whenever you are totalling a range of values. If the cells you are totalling do not involve a range, you might just as well use an ordinary formula.

=SUM(A1:A30,G9) will add together the values in all the cells from A1 through to A30 as well as cell G9. This would be tedious to do in any other way.

=SUM(A1,B2,C3) or =SUM(A1+B2+C3) will each give the same answer, but are more rationally expressed as =A1+B2+C3

=SUM(A1-B3) is silly. It actually works, because you are asking for the sum of a single item (the result of A1-B3), but the SUM() function is quite unnecessary, and it should be entered as =A1-B3

👍 *Use SUM() where a range of numbers is involved, even if it is a very short range (it might grow later); otherwise, use a simple formula.*

AutoSumming Multiple Totals

If you have a range of cells selected, AutoSum has another trick up its sleeve. Consider this slightly modified version of your sheet (you could easily try it if you like):

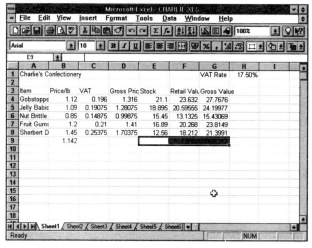

You have added a column of gross retail values, and you are ready to sum all three columns.

Clicking immediately enters all three sums (assuming the 'guess' to be correct):

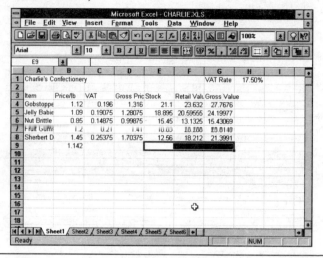

> ☞ *If you want to change this 'guess', just click AutoSum again (with the range of totals still selected).*

🖑 *If you have experimented, clear any unwanted data by selecting cells and pressing ▭*

————The Function Wizard————

There are lots of different functions available in Excel. Initially, using functions may seem daunting. Even the most experienced user will find it hard to remember all of the functions that Excel provides. For this reason, Excel comes with a Function Wizard to help you through the stages involved.

Wizards are a common feature of Microsoft software. They are designed to provide guidance whilst performing actions that, while not necessarily difficult, involve a lot of separate steps. Wizards generally present a series of dialogs, one for each step in the process.

For an example of Function Wizard use, you need a function that is a bit more complicated than SUM() or AVERAGE() – which can easily be typed! You have chosen PMT() – the payment function, used to work out the payment on an annuity, e.g. a mortgage payment. This has nothing to do with the example, but it is interesting to note that if you want to do a quick calculation, unconnected with the sheet you are working on, you can do so using any convenient (empty) cells – and you can clear them afterwards.

Select cell E11 (for the sake of example) and click ⨎ on the Standard toolbar.

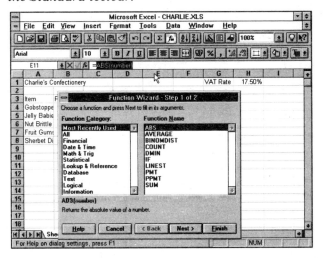

The dialog shows:

- A list of the different categories of functions available; currently the Most Recently Used category is selected.

- A list of the functions in that category; in the case of Most Recently Used, the exact list of Function Names depends on

what functions you have already used, so yours is likely to
be different.

- An illustration of the syntax of the function.
- A one line description of the currently selected function.
- A row of navigation buttons.

The Function Wizard title bar shows 'Step 1 of 2'. These steps
are navigated using the buttons along the bottom of the dialog.
The actions of these buttons should be obvious, though note
that [Finish] accepts all the settings (default or those that you
have made) and completes the Wizard.

PMT() is a Financial function so:

🖰 *Select Financial from the Function Category list box.*

🖰 *Select PMT from the Function Name list box.*

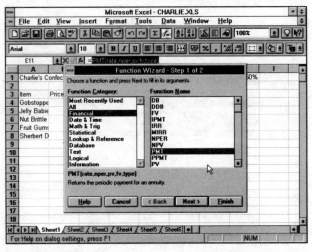

The information line now displays a description of the PMT()
function.

Click Next >

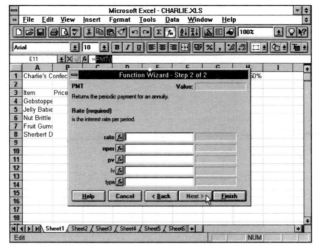

The Wizard moves on to 'Step 2 of 2'. It is now possible to fill in the arguments. The arguments can be entered either by typing in values (as you will do in the first, simple example), or by entering references to cells and ranges that hold the required data (by typing or using the mouse to select the relevant cells).

Mortgage payments are usually made monthly, so you must enter one twelfth of the annual interest rate.

Type the interest rate, e.g.: 11.5%/12

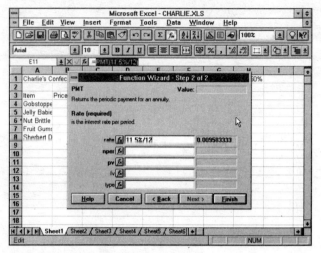

Notice how the value has been worked out for you.

 Press Tab *to move to the next argument (or use the mouse) and type the number of periods. For a 20 year mortgage, this will be 20*12 (1 for each month):*

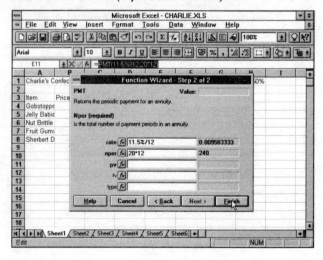

> ᗗᗕᎣᎯ Notice that 🔣 appears next to each of the argument text fields. This
> allows you to use the function Wizard to supply further functions that
> can themselves be arguments to the 'main' function. This **nesting** of
> functions permits complex formulae to be created in a single cell.
> The Function Wizard can be used to 'nest' functions down to seven
> levels.

🖉 *Press* Tab *and enter the amount of borrowing (the present
value), e.g.: 60000*

Notice that you needn't use the £ sign.

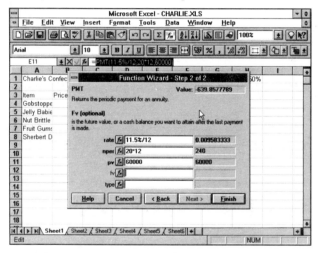

The remaining arguments are optional, as indicated on the
dialog by the fact that the labels are not bold. In this case they
are not needed.

> ᗗᗕᎣᎯ You will have to read an Excel manual, or the help facility, if you
> wish to learn more about these options.

Click 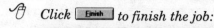 to finish the job:

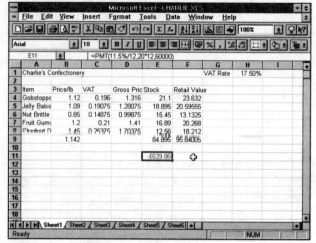

The figure is negative, as it is a payment, whereas the capital sum (the loan) is a receipt.

Warning: this may not be exactly how your mortgage is worked out. Please don't be surprised if this does not predict your own payment to the nearest penny!

The Wizard has helped you enter a function that you haven't used before. As familiarity with certain functions grow, you might dispense with the services of the Wizard – but return to it when dealing with a new one.

Next time you use the Function Wizard, you will find PMT in the Most Recently Used category.

Further note that the Wizard can be invoked whenever you are editing a cell. When you edit a cell, three buttons appear on the Formula Bar:

☒	Clicking this will cause Excel to leave cell edit mode, leaving the cell as it was before it was edited (Esc has the same effect).
☑	Clicking this will cause Excel to leave edit mode, retaining the modifications made to the cell content (pressing Enter has the same effect).
fx	Clicking this will invoke the Function Wizard tool.

As a further example, suppose you wish to find the lowest and highest values in some of your columns, you need two new functions, MAX() and MIN().

⤵ *Select the cell holding your PMT function, and delete it using* ⌫

⤵ *Enter the text* **Lowest** *and* **Highest** *into cells A13 and A14 respectively.*

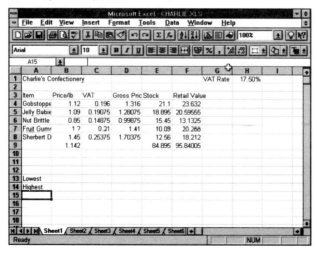

Select cell B13 and use the Function Wizard (click) to enter the MIN() function – it is a Statistical function.

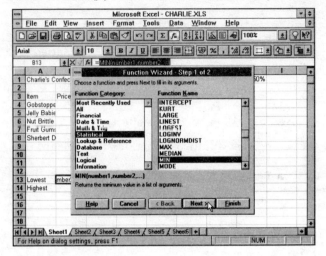

 Click Next >

You will see that this is a simpler function – rather like SUM() or AVERAGE() it simply takes a list of ranges of cells (or single cells).

🖱 *Move the dialog (by dragging its title bar) and drag the mouse so as to select the cells B4:B8 (don't include B9):*

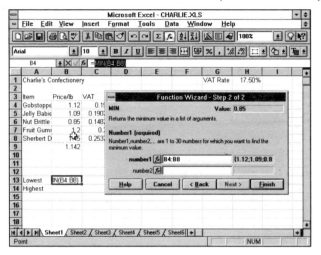

That's all you need for this one.

🖱 *Click* [Finish]

That was an easy function and you might simply remember it and type it in future.

As a final example, suppose you get part way through entering a function, and you forget what the argument is.

🖱 *Select B14 and type =MAX(and press* [Ctrl] [Shift] [A]

This has inserted the argument, and is sometimes all you need.

🖱 *Press* [Esc] *and start again, this time pressing* [Ctrl] [A]

This takes you straight to step 2 of the Function Wizard, using the function name in the current cell (provided it is recognised). Using either of these methods you can complete the job by selecting the range concerned: B4:B8.

Notice that 'max' has been capitalised (if you typed it in lowercase), showing that Excel has accepted it as a valid function name. If Excel had not recognised the function name, nothing would have happened.

🖱 *Select the appropriate range and click* <kbd>Finish</kbd> *(or press* <kbd>Enter</kbd> *twice).*

👈 *Notice that if you use the* <kbd>Ctrl</kbd> <kbd>Shift</kbd> <kbd>A</kbd> *method, you have to delete any unwanted arguments before completing your function.*

🖱 *Use the Fill handle (twice) to enter the functions in the other cells:*

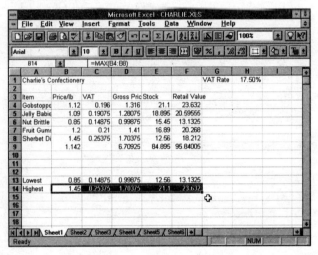

Summary: Functions

- Excel has many built-in functions which are used to perform calculations and return results.
- Σ inserts the Sum function into a cell, guessing the range to be summed.
- All functions can be entered either by typing them directly or using the Function Wizard 🔣 .
- Ctrl A may be used to call step 2 (arguments) of the Function Wizard when entering functions manually.
- Ctrl Shift A may be used to insert the argument list into the formula in the formula bar.
- Individual cell references and ranges may be inserted into the argument list by pointing and dragging as well as by typing

7

FORMATTING

This chapter covers:

- Inserting rows.
- Applying cell formats, including borders, text and number formatting.
- Making multiple selections.
- Altering column widths.

In the previous chapters you have been building a spreadsheet for Charlie's Confectionery. If you have a saved version of it, from the previous exercises, you could open it now:

🖑 *Click* 🖻, *select the drive and directory in which you saved your work, select* CHARLIE.XLS *(or whatever you called it) and click* ⬛ **OK** ⬛

Whether you are working with an existing sheet or not, you will need to spend a few moments making your sheet look something like the example below (using the techniques explained earlier in the book).

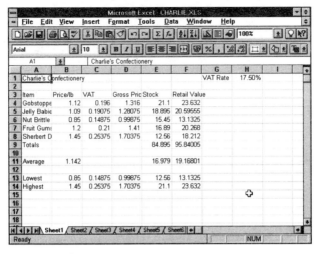

Points to remember:

- Type in titles, like **Average**

- Once a formula has been entered in one cell, it can be copied to adjacent cells using the Fill handle (see Chapter 4), e.g. F4 into F5:F8.

- You can move cells by dragging the range boundary (see Chapter 4), e.g. you have moved the Average calculation from B9 to B11.

- Copy cells by dragging the range boundary whilst holding `Ctrl`, e.g. you have copied the average calculation to cells E11 and E12.

───── **Inserting rows** ─────

Suppose that Charlie has started a new line of sweets called UFOs. Adding it to the end of the current list would make a mess of the line of totals, so you might prefer to insert a new row somewhere in the middle.

Select the whole of row 6 by clicking the grey row 6 heading on the left hand side.

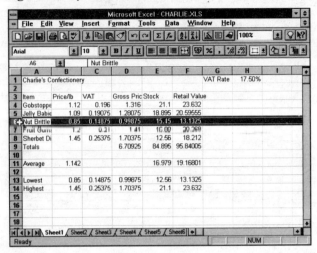

From the _Insert_ menu, select _Rows_ (or right-click the row heading and choose Insert from the resulting shortcut menu or press Ctrl +).

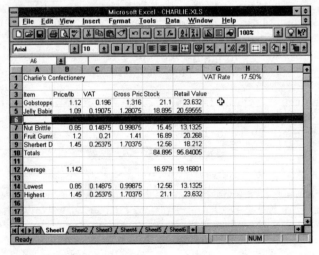

Excel has now inserted a whole new row into the spreadsheet. Helpfully, Excel has adjusted the formulae in the spreadsheet to allow for the new row. You can check this by examining a formula, for example the one now in cell F10. F10 used to hold =SUM(F4:F8), it now holds =SUM(F4:F9).

Had you inserted a row at row 1 of your sheet, the formula would have become =SUM(F5:F9). Confusion can arise when you are near the boundary of your table: a row inserted at row 4 does **not** get included in your formula.

 *Enter* **UFOs** *into cell A6, and* **.75** *into cell B6:*

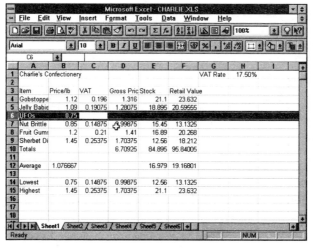

Adding the calculated fields of VAT and selling price is simple. The Fill handle can be used to copy the appropriate formulae from the cells above (or below).

✏ *Use the Fill handle to enter the cell contents in row 6 for 'VAT' and 'Selling Price' (select the cells above and then drag the Fill handle down).*

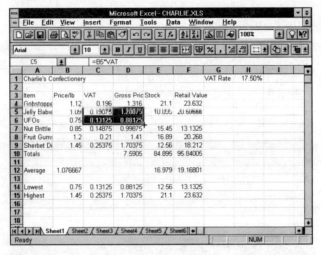

✏ *Enter 25 as the amount of stock in cell E6.*

✏ *Use the Fill handle again to enter the 'Value of Stock' formula for UFOs.*

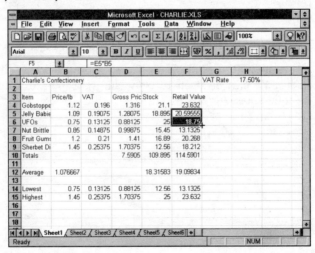

Notice that the totals at the bottom of the sheet now take account of the Stock and Stock Value totals for UFOs. Excel adjusted the formulae to allow for the row insertion, expanding the range of cells for the Sum calculations.

Columns can be inserted in an analogous way.

Deleting Rows

Rows, and columns, can be deleted too.

🖱 *Select the whole of row 11 by clicking the grey row 11 heading on the left hand side.*

🖱 *From the Edit menu, select Delete (or right-click the row heading and choose Delete from the resulting shortcut menu or press [Ctrl] [-]).*

🖱 *Delete the new row 12, to give:*

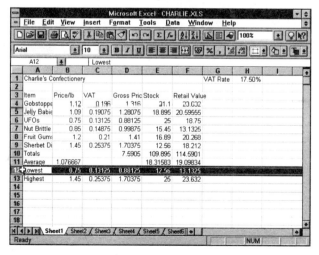

Further methods of deleting and inserting rows and columns will be explored later.

AutoFormat

The AutoFormat feature of Excel allows you to choose a format for a table of data from a previously defined list of formats. It is very quick and often very effective. Later in this chapter we go on to explain how you can choose exactly the format you want, item by item.

When you use the AutoFormat feature, make sure that either you have the whole table selected, or merely one cell within the table concerned. If you have a few cells selected, the AutoFormat will be applied only to those cells; if you have a single cell selected, Excel 'guesses' the area of interest.

In fact, Excel selects the 'Current Region', which is the range (containing the active cell) which is surrounded by empty cells. You can select the current region yourself using Ctrl *.*

With any single cell (within the table of data) selected, take the AutoFormat... option from the Format menu:

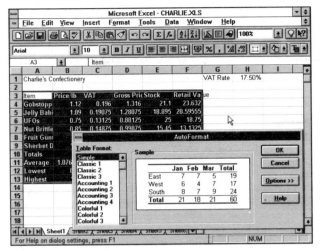

You can use ⬆ and ⬇ to choose an AutoFormat. AutoFormats include colours, number formatting, font effects and so on.

Press Options >> :

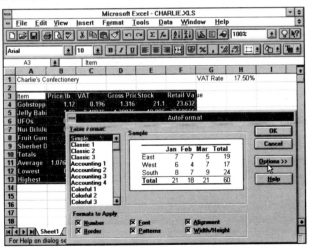

You will see that a number of effects of the AutoFormats
can be switched off – e.g. you might want column widths
altering, but no patterns (colours and shading):

Option	Examples
Number	Some AutoFormats change the number of decimal places displayed
Font	Effects like Bold and Italics
Alignment	In this example, most of the headings in row 3 will be centred within their cells.
Borders	Lines around cells
Patterns	Colours and shadings
Width/Height	In this example, the width of columns will be changed so as nicely to accommodate the data within the columns

Select a format you like, and click [OK]:

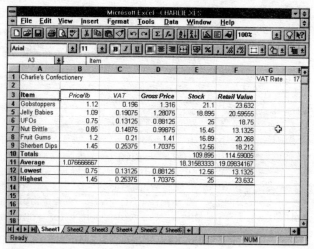

Press Ctrl Z to undo the effect.

☝ *If you don't like your AutoFormat, use* `Ctrl` `Z` *immediately to undo it. Once you have done something else, you won't be able to undo the AutoFormat.*

Actually there is the option to set AutoFormat to 'none', but this will not undo changes to column widths (for example).

✐ *Try out some other AutoFormats, undoing them immediately in each case.*

If you end up not being able to undo an AutoFormat, simply choose the 'none' option from the AutoFormat list.

The value of AutoFormat

AutoFormat has made a pretty good job of improving the look of your example, and you may take the view that this is good enough for you. It is likely, though, that sooner or later you will have a sheet that is so complicated that AutoFormat won't cope with it, or that you simply won't be able to find the effect you are seeking. So the rest of this chapter (and the next chapter) is devoted to formatting features, many of which are the building blocks of AutoFormat.

——Using the Formatting toolbar——

The Formatting toolbar, introduced earlier, offers quick access to many features designed to enhance the appearance of Excel data, e.g. bold, italics, borders and number formats. In this section, the appearance of the worksheet will be improved using some of these tools. Of course, it would be possible to use the Format menu, but this is only necessary for some of the more esoteric options.

The Border tool

🖑 *Select cells A3:F3.*

The Border tool ⊞▣ is unusual in that it is in two parts. The larger, left side shows the latest formatting applied using the button, or initially the default. This formatting can be applied by using the left side of the button. On the right is a drop-down arrow. Clicking this will produce a palette of border choices.

🖑 *Click the drop-down button on the Border tool*

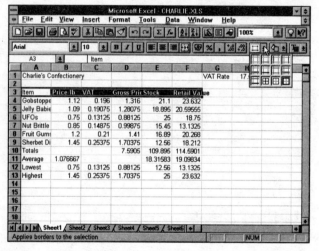

The palette displayed offers many border format choices, including a complete border, borders for individual sides, and an option at the top left of the palette to remove all borders (dotted lines on any of the sides indicate that no border will be applied to that part of the selection). Any of these options can be applied to the current selection by clicking the relevant box in the palette.

👍 *The gridlines shown on the worksheet at the moment are for guidance only. They will not be printed (unless you select a particular printing option for them to do so.) They should be distinguished from the borders you will be applying here.*

Select the option for a thick border at the bottom of the cells only (you can see the mouse pointer about to select it, above). Select a different cell so that you can see the border clearly:

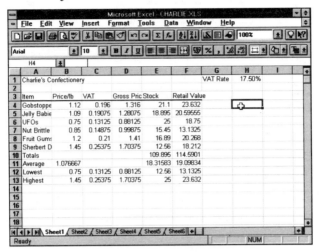

Now, apply a different border to the Totals row.

 Select cells A10:F10.

The palette that you saw attached to the border tool a moment ago can be detached (it is referred to as a 'tear-off palette'). The palette then 'floats' over your worksheet, remaining available, and this may make things easier if you want to apply several borders to a worksheet.

🖑 *Click the Border tool drop-down button and then position your mouse pointer at the edge of the Border drop down palette.*

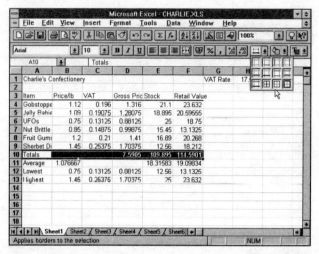

🖑 *Drag the outline (or middle) of the palette away from the toolbar and into the worksheet.*

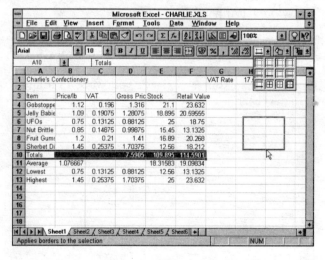

When you have moved the outline into a 'clear' area of the worksheet (so as not to cover your work), let go of the mouse button and the Border palette will appear as a toolbar in its own right.

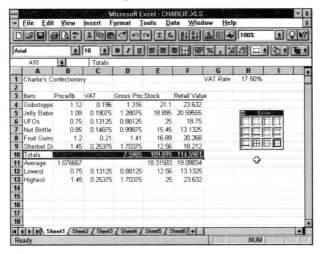

Use the Border palette to put top and bottom borders on the selected cells. Again, click a blank cell to view the change.

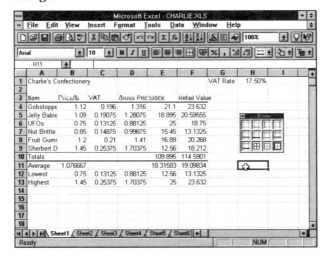

🖐 *Use the same techniques to apply a lower border to the range A13:F13 – 'remember: select then do'.*

When you have finished with the Border palette you might want to hide it again:

🖐 *Click the control box* 🔲 *at the top left of the Border palette to put it away.*

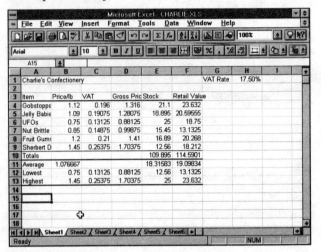

Text formatting

Those familiar with word processing will be used to the idea of applying text formatting. For example, you might want to make a title stand out by applying a bold format. You might emphasise some other text using italics. You could also use different fonts or different sizes. All of these options are possible in Excel, including the option to format a character or characters forming part of the cell's display rather than the cell display text as a whole.

For instance, to make the names of the sweets stand out, you could italicise them.

Select cells A4:A9.

Apply italic format to these cells by clicking ▣ on the Formatting toolbar (⌘Ctrl⌘ I also works).

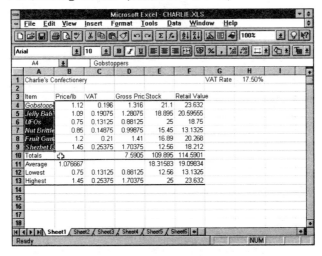

Multiple selections

It is often useful to be able to apply a command to a selection of cells which are not in a single range, and therefore cannot be selected by a simple click and drag. However, you can make a multiple selection by holding down Ctrl while making the second and subsequent selections.

Multiple selections could be employed here in making both the table headings and the Total cells bold.

Select cells A3:F3

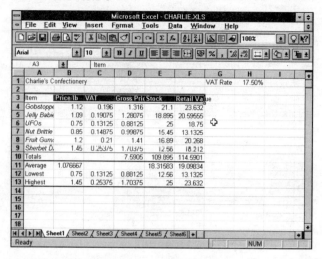

Hold down Ctrl *and select cells A10:F10*

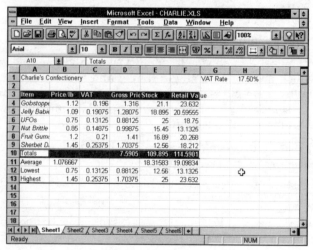

Click **B** *on the Formatting toolbar. Select a blank cell to deselect the row and see the change clearly.*

	A	B	C	D	E	F	G	H	I
1	Charlie's Confectionery						VAT Rate	17.50%	
2									
3	Item	Price/lb	VAT	Gross Price	Stock	Retail Value			
4	Gobstoppe	1.12	0.196	1.316	21.1	23.632			
5	Jelly Babie	1.09	0.19075	1.28075	18.895	20.59555			
6	UFOs	0.75	0.13125	0.88125	25	18.75			
7	Nut Brittle	0.85	0.14875	0.99875	15.45	13.1325			
8	Fruit Gums	1.2	0.21	1.41	16.89	20.268			
9	Sherbert L	1.45	0.25375	1.70375	12.56	18.212			
10	Totals				109.895	114.5901			
11	Average	1.076667			18.31583	19.09834			
12	Lowest	0.75	0.13125	0.88125	12.56	13.1325			
13	Highest	1.45	0.25375	1.70375	25	23.632			
14									
15									
16									
17									
18									

You may prefer to use keystrokes to apply bold and italic formatting. The keystroke for bold is ⌈Ctrl⌋⌈B⌋ and for italic it is ⌈Ctrl⌋⌈I⌋

——— Altering column widths ———

It is often the case that the cell result is too large to fit inside the default column width. Chapter 4 explained how to re-size a column to be just as wide as necessary for display – 'best fit'. It is also possible to re-size a column to fit the widest cell within a selection.

If Column A were to be re-sized as a whole, it would become as wide as the display for the title in cell A1. You might think this to be undesirable: it is only be necessary for the column to be widened enough to display the items in the table. The title text in cell A1 doesn't need extra display space, because B1 is blank and can be overwritten by A1.

Select cells A3:A13

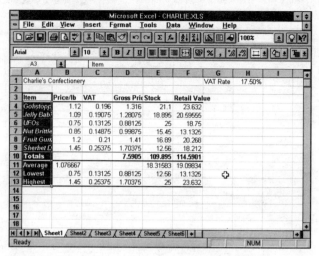

Choose F̲ormat, C̲olumn, A̲utoFit Selection.

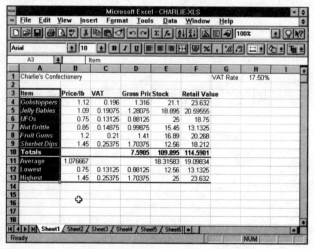

You can best fit Column B as a whole (remember the title is only 'borrowing' B1's display space).

Move the mouse pointer between the headings for columns
B and C, where you should see the **↔** mouse pointer. With
↔ showing, double-click.

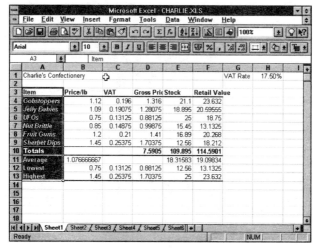

You might feel that the number of decimal places used for the
averages is extreme – we will deal with this shortly.

It is also possible to best fit more than one column at a time. To
do this you select all the columns and then best fit one of them
– this automatically best fits the others also.

Select columns C to F by dragging across their headings.

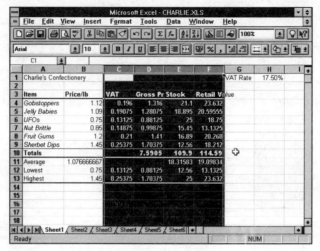

Position the mouse pointer between the headings for any two columns (e.g. columns F and G) and double-click.

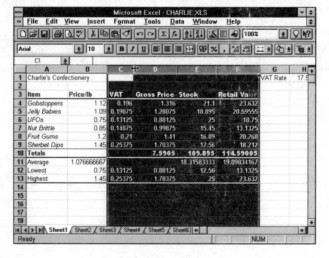

Summary: Formatting

- Extra rows or columns can be added to a spreadsheet by selecting rows or columns and using the Insert Rows or Insert Columns command (or ⌈Ctrl⌉⌈+⌉).

- Rows and columns can be removed by selecting them and using Edit Delete (or ⌈Ctrl⌉⌈-⌉).

- The Formatting toolbar can be used to change the font and size of text in cells, and to apply bold, italic or underline to them.

- The border tool ⌈⊞⌉ can be used to add a variety of border formats to cells.

- ✛ can be used to re-size columns, double-clicking best-fits.

- The Format Column AutoFit selection can be used to re-size a column to the width of the widest cell in a selection.

8

MORE FORMATTING

This chapter covers:

- Shortcut menus for formatting cells.
- Changing colours of cells.
- Centring text in cells.
- Number formatting.
- Using the Format Painter tool.

——Shortcut menus for formatting——

Earlier chapters have introduced the concept of right-clicking to produce a shortcut menu. There is a shortcut option for performing cell formatting.

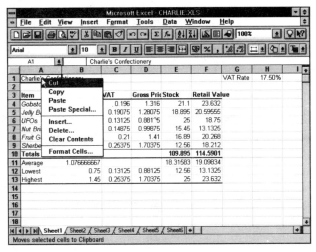

Right-click cell A1

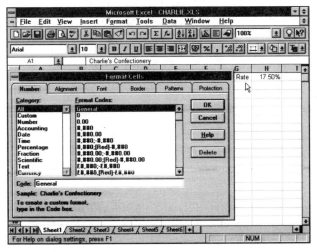

Select *Format Cells...* from the Shortcut menu.

This is the same dialog as would be accessed by choosing Cells from the Format menu. There are six tabs here, each relating to different aspects of cell formatting:

Tab	Purpose
Font	Font formatting (bold, italic, font, size etc.)
Alignment	Text alignment and orientation
Border	Cell borders (covered in chapter)
Patterns	Cell colours and patterns (shadings)
Number	Number formatting (currency, date, etc.)
Protection	Allows cells to be locked against editing and/or hidden

☞ *Click the Font tab in this dialog.*

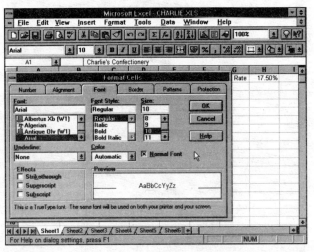

This tab offers you many text formatting options, not just those to change the font. You can use the scroll bars to view the available fonts, font styles and font sizes. Underline and Color have their own drop-down lists. The Effects section contains options for Strikethrough (useful for displaying text as 'old' or 'cancelled'), and Superscript or Subscript.

☞ *Make the text Times New Roman, Bold, 14pt and green, with a single underline.*

 *Click* OK

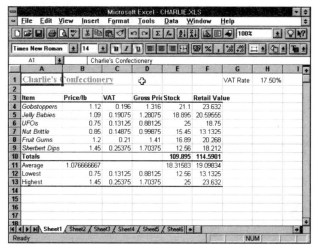

Colours

In addition to changing the colour of text in cells (which, incidentally can be done from the Font Colour palette on the formatting toolbar). , it is also possible to change the colour of the cells themselves.

 *Select cells A1:F1.*

Although the Patterns tab of the Format Cells... dialog could be used for this task, it is quicker to use the Color tool [⬛] on the Formatting toolbar. In fact the change of font colour could also have been done from the toolbar.

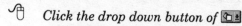

Click the drop down button of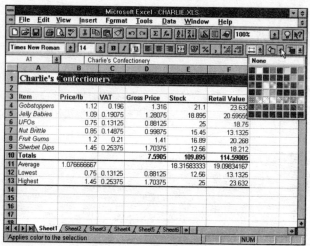

This palette will also 'tear off', if desired.

Select a dark blue colour.

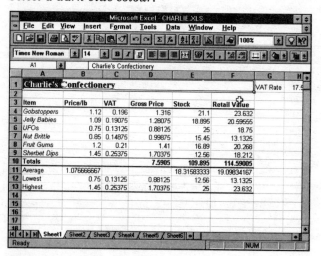

Note that, from the Border tab of the F̲ormat C̲e̲lls... dialog,
you can set the colour of border lines.

—— Centring a title across columns ——

It is possible to align text within cells using ▦▦▦. However, here, it is sometimes desirable to be able to centre text across several columns – e.g. the Charlie's Chocolates heading across all six columns of your table. This is done using ▦. This tool should not be confused with ▦, which merely centres text within a particular cell.

With cells A1:F1 (still) selected, click ▦

Click a blank cell to view the new formatting.

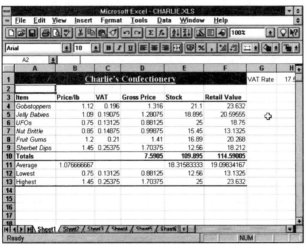

Notice that, although the text appears to be in cells C and D, it is still in cell A1. The text in A1 is formatted to appear elsewhere, and any changes to the width of columns A, B, C, D, E or F will cause the title to be re-centred.

Number formatting

As well as applying formatting to the text, it is possible to format the display of numbers, for example, with a currency symbol, or to a certain number of decimal places. By default, every cell in the sheet has the **General format** (number format) applied. In General format, Excel will choose a *reasonable* way of displaying a number; it may not format the numbers exactly as you would choose.

In General format, numbers are displayed up to a limit of 11 digits in total (including a decimal point as a digit) with as many decimal places as required up to the total digit limit.

> *Beyond this, very large or very small numbers are displayed in scientific notation (1E+6 which represents 1 multiplied by 10^6, i.e. 1,000,000 – similarly, 1E-6 represents 0.000001) in the same way that most calculators do when displaying very large or very small numbers. Some infamous examples might be the speed of light (3E8 ms^{-1}, i.e. 300,000,000) and the charge on a electron (1.6E-19 C, i.e. 0.00000000000000000016). Clearly, scientific notation is quite useful is some situations!*

is used to apply Currency formatting to numbers, for example: £10.00

applies Comma formatting, i.e. thousands separated by commas. For example: 1,536,422.00

applies Percent formatting, for example: 12.75%, which displays 0.1275 as 12.75%

Many of the figures in this spreadsheet represent money. It would be useful for the cell formatting to reflect this.

Select cells F4:F13 and click [image] on the Formatting tool-bar.

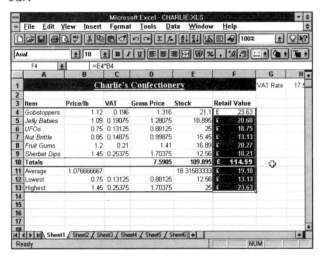

Decimal places

Those cells displaying numbers that have not been formatted as currency are still formatted in General format and are therefore showing up to nine decimal places.

Whilst Charlie wants to record his actual stock values as accurately as his scales allow, he does not need to see the detailed figures on the sheet. Perhaps you'd like to see two decimal places in the Stock column. The Decrease Decimal ([image]) and Increase Decimal ([image]) tools can be used to format selected cells to display the required number of decimal places. It is important to note that the numbers are still stored with a far higher accuracy than is generally displayed: you are only adjusting how they are displayed.

> ✍ *Numbers are stored to a very high accuracy: around 15 decimal places, even though only they may displayed with less accuracy. For a number you've typed in, e.g. 1.12 this is not really an issue, because you'd probably display it as 1.12. For a calculated number, like the average in cell A11, which you might display with 2 decimal places, the number displayed would then be rounded from the real number, e.g. 1.12346 would be rounded to 1.12, and 1.1567 would be rounded to 1.16*

🖰 *Select cells E4:E13 and click* 🔢

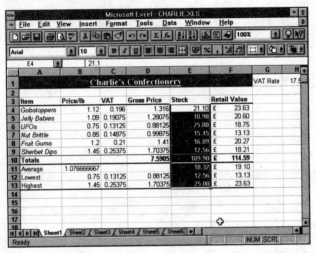

This causes the active cell to display an extra decimal place, subsequently bringing the other selected cells into line, so that they show the same number of decimal places as the active cell.

Click 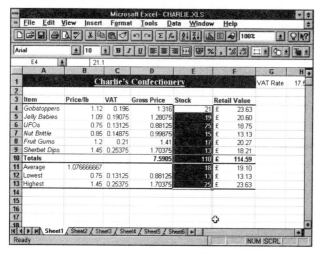 *twice.*

The column now shows a consistent and reasonable number of decimal places.

——————The Format Painter tool——————

For uniformity with the cells to which they refer, other cells containing currency would look better if formatted with the currency style and any other formats that you may have applied to your cells. You could just use ⊞ again, but if other formats had also been applied, you would have to repeat those as well. Therefore, it is often simpler to copy the formatting from the cells you adjusted. The Format Painter (⊠) provides a way of doing this.

Select cell F4, then click ☑ (note the special mouse pointer shape that results).

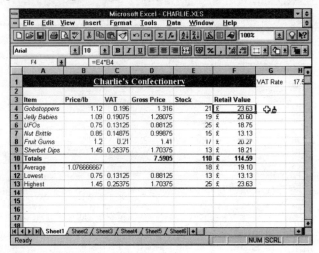

The mouse pointer is 'loaded' with the formatting of cell F4. It is now possible to 'paint' this formatting onto another cell or range of cells.

Apply this format to cells B4:B9 by dragging over the range.

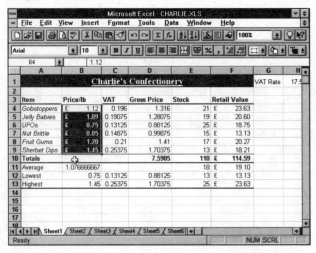

Clicking the Format Painter once allows you to perform a single format pasting operation. Multiple format painting is possible by double-clicking the Format Painter tool.

🖰 *Select cell F4 and double-click*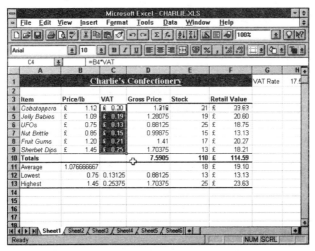

🖰 *Paint this format to cells C4:C9.*

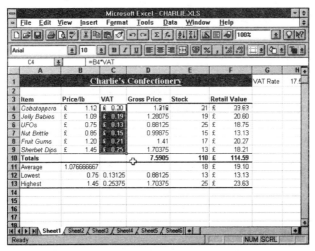

You can continue formatting other cells with the same format without having to reactivate the Format Painter.

Apply the format to cells D4:D9 by selecting them.

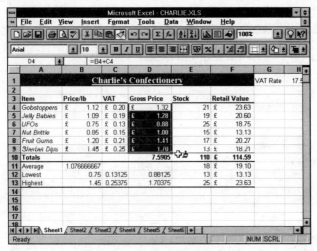

Finally, apply the format to cells B11:D13

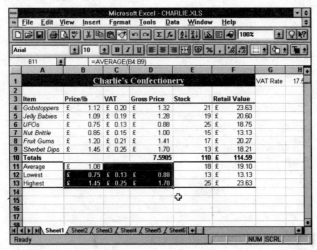

When you have finished applying formatting it is important not to forget to cancel the Format Painter. If you do forget and make another selection before cancelling, those cells will have the selected format applied to them.

🖰 *To cancel the selection, click the Format Painter tool or press* Esc

👍 *Selecting another command or tool before making a cell selection will cancel the operation of the Format Painter tool. However, it is better practice to cancel the Format Painter overtly.*

🖰 *Deselect the range by clicking cell E15.*

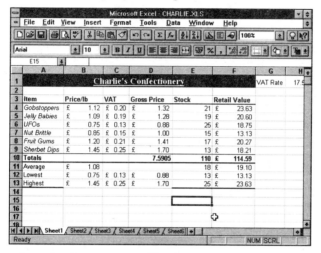

Notice that the lowermost cells that you just formatted have 'lost' their bottom border. This is because cell F4 that you copied from has no bottom border and when you copied cell F4 you copied <u>all</u> the formats of that cell.

To get the border back you will need to format-paint cell F13 onto B13:E13.

Select F13, click 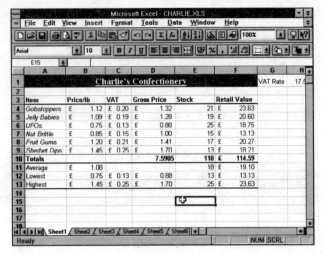 and select B13:D13.

Dates

It is frequently useful to include the current date in a spreadsheet. In this section, you will see two ways of doing this in Excel. The methods provide distinct results: the differences are discussed below.

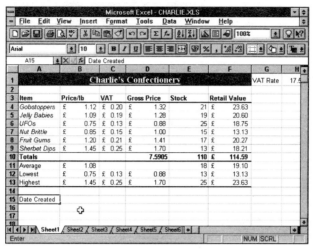 *Type* **Date Created** *into cell A15.*

The keystroke <kbd>Ctrl</kbd> <kbd>;</kbd> puts today's date into a cell.

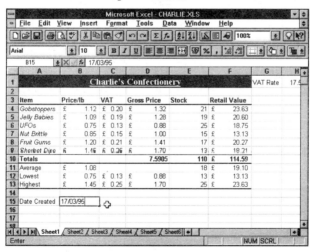 *Select cell B15 and press* <kbd>Ctrl</kbd> <kbd>;</kbd>

This puts the current date into the selected cell, just as if you'd typed it.

The date and time are entered in the default system format. Control over these defaults is available from the International icon in the Windows Control Panel.

You still need to enter the date as the contents of this cell.

 Press Enter

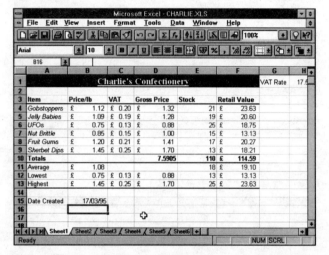

There is another way of putting the date into a cell. The function 'Today' will always recalculate and display the current date, rather than the date on which it was entered.

Enter =TODAY() *into cell B16.*

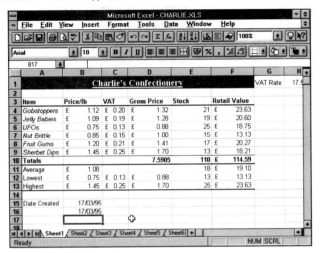

The function =TODAY() also enters today's date. However, as a function, it will be re-calculated by Excel. Therefore if you were to open up the worksheet tomorrow, the function would reflect the new date, whereas cell B15 will not be updated. Note: the brackets are essential.

Suppose you want only a record of the date when the worksheet was created. Therefore, a date that will not be updated is required. To delete the unwanted date function:

 Select cell B16 and choose Edit Clear All.

 For the next part of this exercise to work correctly, it is important that you Clear All.

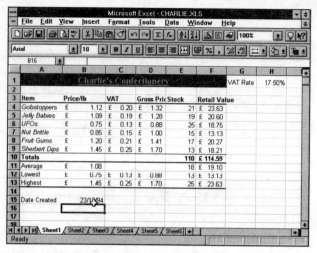

There is another, similar, function called 'Now', which gives the date and time.

Type `Date Printed` *into cell A16 and* `=Now()` *into cell B16.*

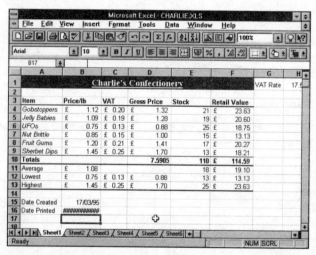

Surprisingly, the date is apparently entered as a series of hash marks (#)! But there is no need to panic: these symbols simply mean that there is a number in this cell (dates are considered by Excel to be numbers) that is too wide to be displayed in the cell. You may remember that this cell was reduced in size when you performed a best fit on the columns a little earlier. You can now make the column wide enough to display the date either by double-clicking the boundary between the heading blocks for columns B and C as above, or you could select the cell with the date in it and choose Format Column AutoFit Selection (the date is the widest thing in this column).

Use one of these methods to best-fit the column width (for column B).

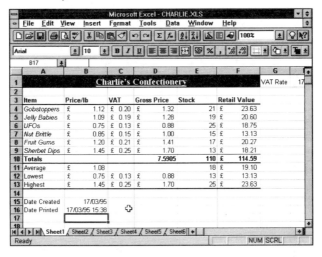

Summary: More formatting

- Cells can be formatted quickly using shortcut menus (obtained by right-clicking)
- ⬛ changes the background colour of cells.
- ⬛ enables easy centring of a title across several columns.
- It is possible to change the number of decimal places displayed using the appropriate tools, i.e. ⬛ and ⬛
- The Format Painter ⬛ allows a given format to be re-applied to other cells quickly and easily.
- You can enter the current date so that it automatically updates or so that it is fixed.

9

SAVING

This chapter covers:
- Saving a workbook.
- Save and Save As.
- The Summary Info dialog.
- File Find.

Saving the workbook

As already covered in chapter 5, your work should be saved regularly. Since this sheet has already been saved (and has a name) clicking 🔲 merely saves it again, under then same name and in the same location.

🖐 *Click* 🔲 *(or press* Ctrl S *)*

Save and Save As

Once a workbook has been named and saved, clicking will save it again. But this dialog can be invoked in future by using File Save As..., allowing you to save the workbook under a different name and/or in a different location:

You are prompted to give the workbook a name and directory location:

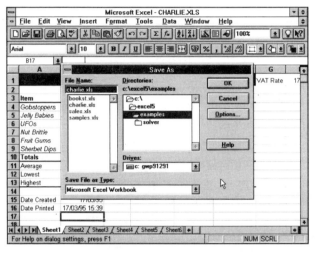

You can use the list boxes to navigate around the drives and directories to choose the most appropriate place for the workbook to be stored. After the document has been saved, you should be returned to your workbook, ready for more editing. For instance, you might like to save this modified version as CHARLIE1.

🖱 *Save your workbook as* CHARLIE1.XLS.

Filenames – a reminder

You may know that in Windows, which runs on top of MS-DOS (on which most users run Windows) you are allowed only up to eight letters for the name and an optional three letters for the extension which comes after a full stop. The name should be unique in the chosen directory. No spaces are allowed.

Certain special characters (including *, / and \) are not allowed in filenames.

We suggest that you restrict your filenames to normal letters and numbers. If you would like to have a space you can use the underscore _ character (for example SALES_94.XLS), which looks quite like a space. Incidentally, you can type filenames in upper or lower case – Excel, like all programs running under Windows, does not distinguish between the two cases and it will accept either.

Updating Summary Info

When you saved the first time you were probably presented with the Summary Info dialog (this actually depends on how Excel is configured – whether or not you have ⊠ Prompt for Summary Info enabled in the General section of the Tools Options dialog). This doesn't happen when you save again, but you can choose File Summary Info... to alter this information.

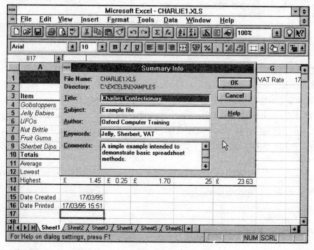

The Summary Info dialog box usually contains text in the Author section. If you want to change this, you can edit and enter new information. However, it is also possible to change the name that appears here as default. To do this choose Tools Options, then alter the User name box in the General tab.

File Find

We will take a few moments here to briefly mention the File Find feature.

It's not always easy to find a file. The File Find facility allows you to search for files using things like: text contained in the file, particular items summary information or files with certain date information.

Take the Find File... option from the File menu:

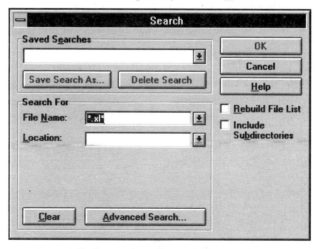

We cannot cover all the options here, but searching for all .XL* files on a particular drive (including subdirectories) will often be all you need (if you wish this to be a fresh file list, not including anything found in previous searches, you should also check the box for Rebuild File List).

🖰 *Choose the location as* C:\ *either by pulling down the Location list and choosing* C:\ *or by typing* C:\ *Also ensure that* ☒ *Include Subdirectories is checked.*

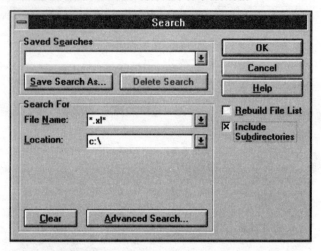

🖰 *Click* OK

On clicking OK (and after a delay):

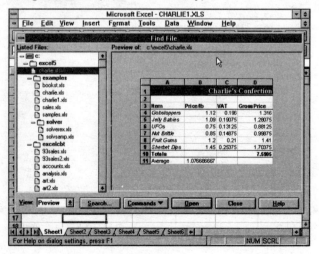

You can preview the first, and open a workbook, or simply close the dialog. There are other commands available:

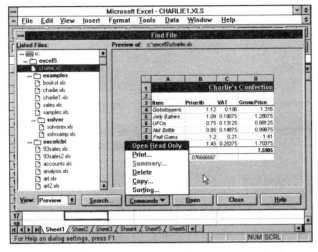

Notice in particular that you can delete unwanted files.

From the original Search dialog, you can go to the advanced search dialog:

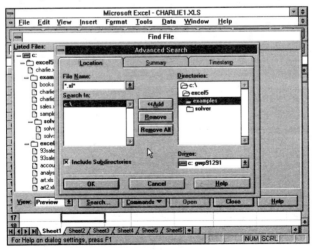

From here you can add a series of paths to be included in the search. From the summary tab:

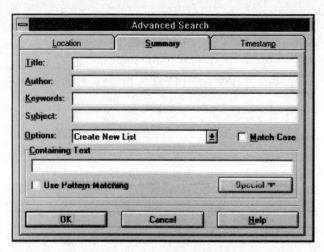

...you can enter any information stored in the summary dialog for your presentation, or even search for any text in the presentation (much slower as it involves reading the entire presentation).

From the Timestamp tab:

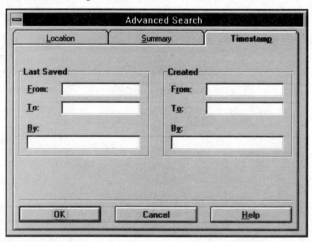

...you can search on the basis of when, and by whom, your presentations were created or last saved.

Summary: Saving

- Workbooks can be saved for later use by using ▣.
- To save a workbook with a different name, or in a different location use File Save As.
- Use the Summary Info dialog to store useful information about your workbook.
- Use File Find to find particular files.

10

── PRINTING ──

This chapter covers:
- Viewing the spreadsheet as it will be printed.
- Changing the margins of the print-out.
- Adding headers and footers.
- Selecting the Print area.

── Print Preview ──

Before printing the worksheet it is advisable to save your work. You may also want to look at a preview of how the printing will come out. Previewing can save lots of time and paper. The Print Preview tool 🔲 on the Standard toolbar will take Excel into preview mode. From here you can access many of the options for controlling the printing of the spreadsheet, and then see their effect.

Click

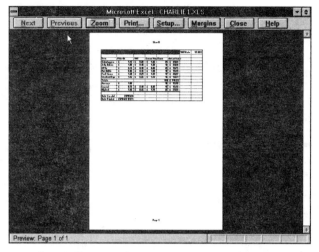

The status bar indicates that you are previewing the first page of your worksheet. You will have noticed that a new toolbar has appeared. The command buttons on it will be reviewed here.

Zoom

One way of getting a closer look at the page would be to click **Zoom**. This will toggle between the normal view and a magnified view of the page. Clicking somewhere on the page will have the same effect.

Click the page to zoom in.

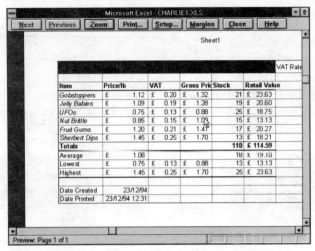

Clicking again anywhere on the page will zoom out.

Margins

Click the display to zoom out then click Margins

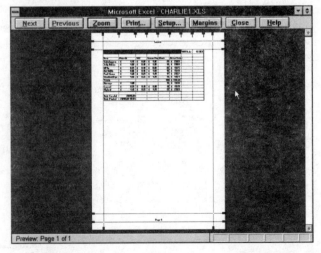

The preview screen now shows a number of black blocks around the edges of the page. These are **handles** and can be used to change the margins, column widths or header and footer area depths (there is more about headers and footers shortly). Some of these handles are attached to dotted lines showing the position of the margins.

To 'grab' a margin line, position the mouse pointer over it so that the pointer shape becomes a double headed arrow (either vertical or horizontal, depending on the margin you are about to change). You can then drag the handle to the desired position. The margin size is given on the status line as you drag the handle to a new position.

Using the above technique, click and drag the left hand margin to about 1.30 inches.

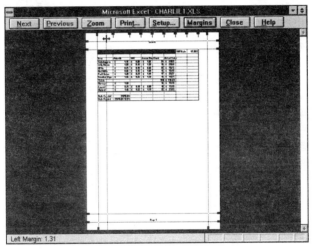

The Page Setup dialog

 *Click* Setup...

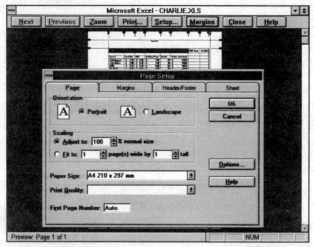

This presents the same dialog that could be reached from the
worksheet via File Page Setup. You are presented with a range
of options for controlling the final output of your work. At the
top of the dialog are four tabs. The Page tab, which you are
looking at now, controls the scaling and orientation of your
output, and the size of paper you wish to print on. By clicking
on the appropriate tab you can set many other options for
printing, such as defining headers and footers, and whether or
not you print sheet gridlines. The margins tab provides another
way of changing your page margins.

> You may notice that certain options on the sheet tab are not avail-
> able when you access the Page Setup dialog via Print Preview.
> These options are available when the menu option (File, Page
> Setup) is used.

🖑 *Click the Margins tab.*

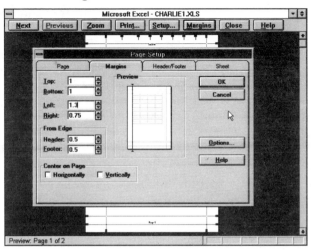

You can type sizes for the margins and choose whether you would like the printing to be centred on the page between those margins.

🖑 *Set the top and bottom margins to 1.5 inches each, and set the table to be centred horizontally and vertically (i.e. to be positioned in the middle of the page).*

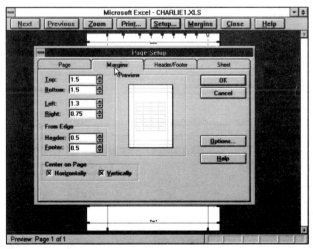

The units of measurement (inches or centimetres) used can be se-lected using the International dialog in the Control Panel window.

Headers and footers

It is possible to make certain information appear on every page: the date, the page number or the name of the worksheet being printed perhaps. This is achieved by setting a header and/or a footer. This will be printed in the space between the edge of the page and the upper and lower margins.

There are several built-in headers and footers. These offer commonly used arrangements of information. There is also the option to customise any of these or to create your own.

 Click the Header/Footer dialog tab.

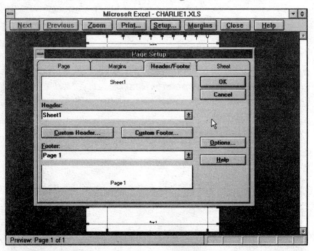

Previews of the header and footer are shown at the top and bottom of this dialog.

🖉 *Click the He_a_der drop-down button.*

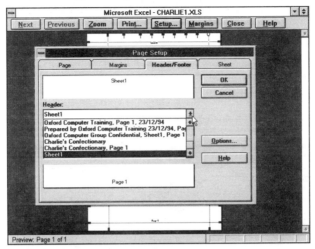

This lists the built-in options available. The different elements of the header are separated by commas. (These commas do not indicate where the elements will be printed on the page.)

🖉 *Choose the option for 'Author, Page No., Date'.*

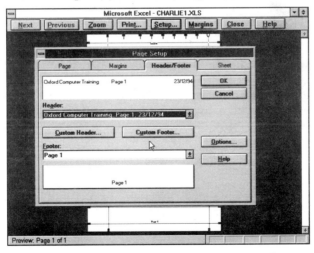

The dialog is currently showing that the page number would be printed in both the header and the footer. Of course, you could remove the page number from the footer, but for this example, assume that you want the name of the worksheet to appear in the header instead of the page number. There is no built-in option encompassing Author, Sheet Name and Date, so to produce the suggested format, it is necessary to customise the header.

Customising the header

 *Click* `Custom Header...`

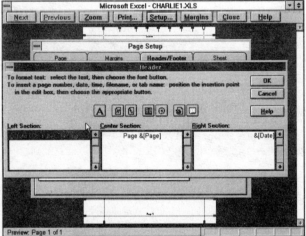

The Centre Section contains the text 'Page' followed by the expression &[Page]. This represents a **field code** which will cause the current page number to be printed. These codes can either be typed or entered using the buttons provided on the dialog.

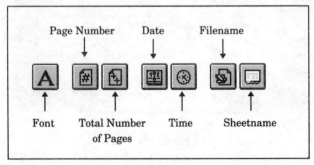

For this example, the contents of the Centre Section are to be replaced with the name of the worksheet being printed.

🖝 *Select the text in the Centre Section.*

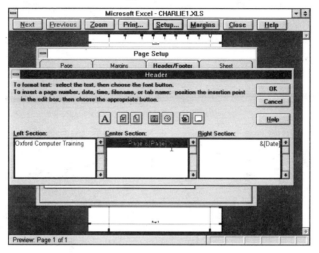

🖝 *Click* ▢

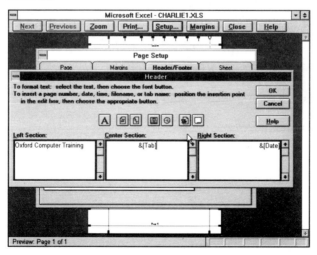

 *Click* OK

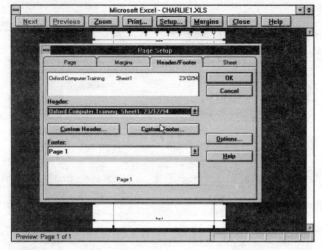

This will cause the name of the current worksheet to be printed in the Centre Section of the Header when this document is printed.

Footers

Footers are designed in much the same way as headers.

 *Click the Footer drop-down button*

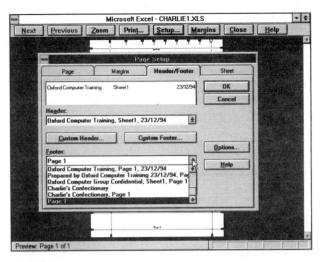

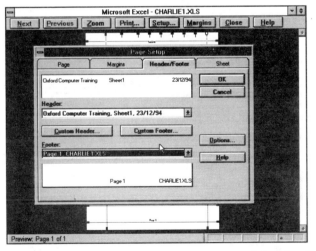 *Choose the 'Page No. ,Workbook Name' option.*

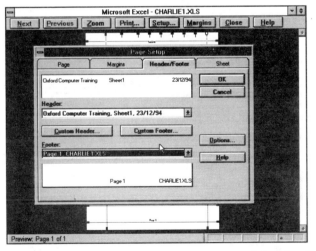

The first element, the page number, is printed in the Centre Section. It would look better if the page number was printed in the Left Section.

Click [Custom Footer...].

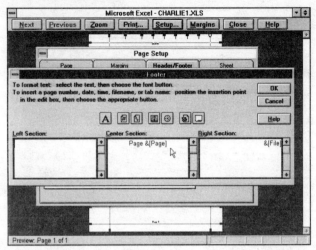

Select the text in the Centre Section.

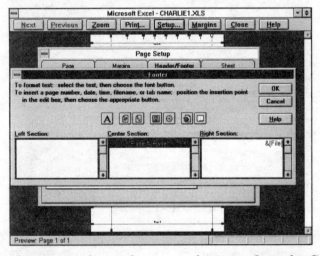

Cut and paste can be used to move the items from the Centre
Section into the Left Section, but you will have to use the keystroke options; there is no access to the tools or the menus
while a dialog is active.

✐ *Press* ⌈Ctrl⌉⌈X⌉ *(the keyboard shortcut for Cut) to remove the information from this section and place it on the clipboard.*

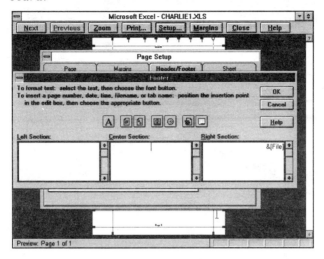

✐ *Click in the* <u>*L*</u>*eft Section and then press* ⌈Ctrl⌉⌈V⌉ *to paste the information cut from the* <u>*C*</u>*entre Section.*

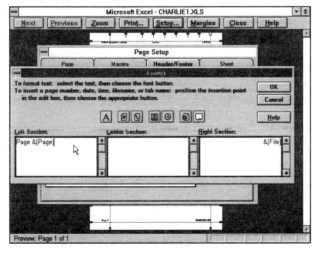

✐ *Click* ⌈ **OK** ⌉

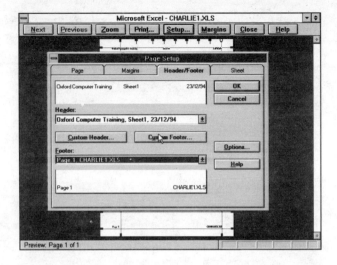

Sheet options

🖑 *Click the Sheet tab.*

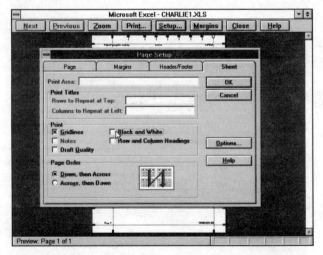

Options here allow control over the order in which the worksheet is printed and the selection of print areas.

If you do not have access to a colour printer, you may find that the colour formatting on your worksheet does not come out very well when rendered in black and white. For this reason, there is an option for Black and White printing. This causes foreground material (such as display text) to be printed as black, and background material to be printed as white, regardless of the colours specified on the worksheet.

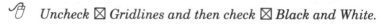 *Uncheck ⊠ Gridlines and then check ⊠ Black and White.*

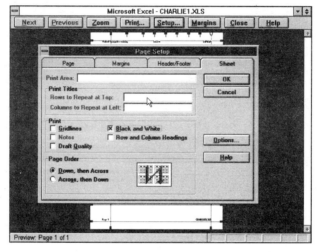

🖱 *Click* OK.

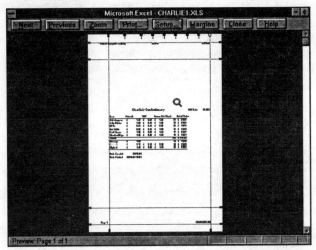

🖱 *Click the display to zoom in for a closer look (you may have to use the scroll bars to see the whole table).*

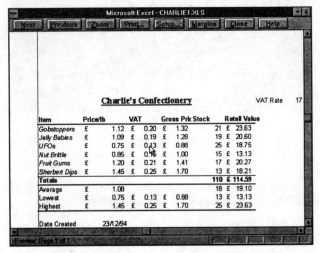

Manual page breaks

So far in this chapter you have been looking at Excel's Print Preview facility, and the options available to us when using this facility. Manual page breaks, on the other hand, can only be inserted or deleted when in normal view.

Excel inserts automatic page breaks as necessary, applying the paper size, orientation and margins specified by the user. On occasion, you may find it helpful to insert your own page breaks. This can be done by positioning the active cell where the page break is required and choosing Insert Page Break. A page break will be inserted at the top left-hand corner of the active cell.

To remove a manual page break, position the active cell anywhere on the row beneath a horizontal page break, or in the column to the right of a vertical page break. Then choose Insert Remove Page Break.

———— Printing the worksheet ————

You are now ready to print your spreadsheet. You can print your work from within Print Preview. It is also possible to print it from the normal spreadsheet view, using File Print or the Print tool 🖨 on the Standard toolbar.

There is a slight difference between these three methods – selecting 🔲 Print... when in Print Preview is identical to using File Print, whereas the 🖨 button will take a short cut and print directly without prompting us with a dialog box. For this example you can print from Print Preview.

Click **Print...**

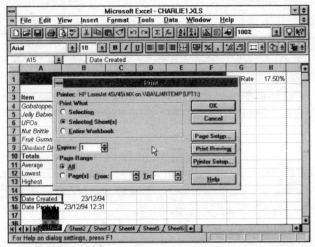

The top line of this dialog tells you which printer the output will be sent to. This is the Windows default printer.

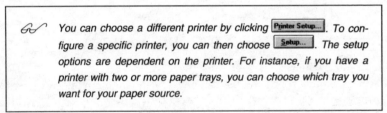

You can choose a different printer by clicking **Printer Setup...**. To configure a specific printer, you can then choose **Setup...**. The setup options are dependent on the printer. For instance, if you have a printer with two or more paper trays, you can choose which tray you want for your paper source.

The rest of the dialog gives you more precise control over what exactly you wish to print out. You can choose either the current selection of cells, the currently selected worksheets, or the entire workbook (Workbooks will be covered in a later chapter). If this will involve more than one page of output, you can choose to print either all pages, or a particular page range. You can also print more than one copy.

If you wish to print the worksheet, click [OK]*, otherwise click* [Cancel]

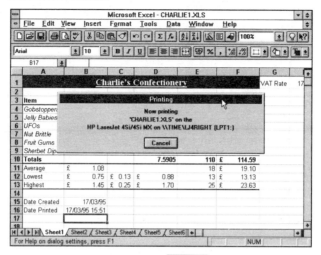

To abort printing, you can click [Cancel] at any time. When the printing has finished, the Printing dialog disappears.

> In a standard Windows setup, Excel does not send the output directly to the printer. Instead, it is sent to an application called the Print Manager, which will then send it on to the appropriate printer. It may still be possible to cancel printing even after Excel has finished by switching to the Print Manager and removing the output from the printer queue. Further opportunities may be available if you are printing to a printer on a network.

Remember, if you want to go straight to printing without going through the print dialog, you can click 🖨 from the Standard toolbar. This prints using the current settings from the print dialog.

Summary: Printing

- Print Preview can be used to check what the printed worksheet will look like before a printed version is produced.
- The Page Setup dialog allows you to specify how you want the printout to look.
- Built-in Headers and Footers are available, although you can also specify your own.
- You can set up your own page breaks.
- You can choose what you want to print from the Print dialog. You can print several copies at once.

11

——— CHARTING ———

This chapter covers:
- Creating a simple chart using The Chart Wizard.
- Adding titles to a chart.
- Changing the chart type.
- Manipulating elements of the chart (e.g. legend, formatting, titles)

——— Creating a chart ———

Creating a chart is much easier than many people imagine, particularly if you are prepared to let Excel use its standard chart styles and accept guidance from the Chart Wizard. Nevertheless, Excel does provide an immense range of charting options for the more adventurous. Many users will find that the default styles combined with a little knowledge will allow them all the flamboyance they require. The **Chart Wizard** provides a 'point and click' guide to selecting the options, together with a preview facility to help you judge the effect of the options you select.

The Chart Wizard

As an example, you're going to create a chart illustrating the varying price per pound of the individual sweets sold by Charlie's Confectionery, using the example created in the earlier chapters.

🖑 *If necessary, open the file* CHARLIE.XLS *(or* CHAR-LIE1.XLS, *depending on the name you chose earlier).*

🖑 *Select cells A3:B9 (i.e. the labels and cost/lb)*

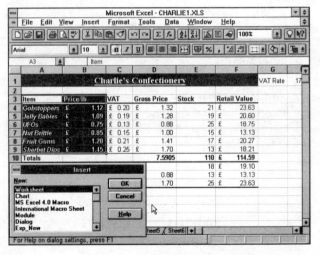

Right-click the Sheet1 tab and choose Insert.

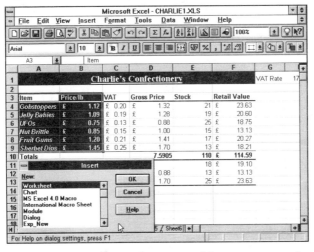

Excel allows you to create charts as either separate sheets or embedded into your worksheet. The following method will create the chart on a new chart sheet in the workbook.

 Choose Chart from the resulting dialog and click **OK**

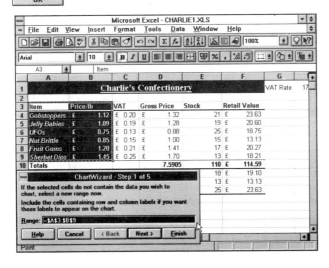

The Chart Wizard immediately appears. Step 1 of the Chart Wizard appears, the first of 5 steps. This step asks you whether you have selected the correct data and gives you the opportunity to re-select. However, in this case, the correct range has been selected.

At the bottom of the dialog are several buttons.

Help	Activates the Help application, to a page explaining the current options.
Cancel	Exits the Chart Wizard without creating a chart.
< Back	Takes you back to the previous step.
Next >	Takes you on to the next step.
Finish	Accepts the options as currently set and applies default options for steps that have not been reached. It then creates the chart.

In this case, Excel has 'picked up' on the selected range and is assuming that this is the source data for the chart – it is, so there is no need to change anything at this step of the Wizard, so you can move on to the next step.

Click

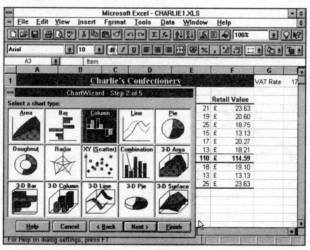

Here, a selection of chart types is offered. Excel can produce charts in both two and (pseudo) three dimensional style – with fifteen chart types available in total. It can also combine two chart types within a single two-dimensional chart.

> 🖘 *The Doughnut chart type is new to Excel 5: it shows the proportion that each item contributes to the whole and, unlike pie charts, it can show more than one data series.*

A simple column chart is appropriate here. This should be the default option in this dialog.

🖑 *If necessary, select the box for Column and click* Next > *(alternatively, double-click the box for Column).*

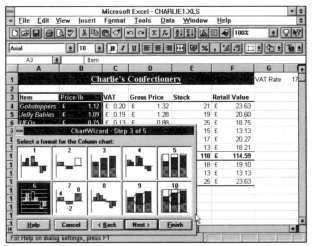

You are not confined to a single column chart type. There are ten to choose from, including different ways of displaying more than one series of data in the same column chart. In this example, there is only one data series, the cost per pound of the sweets. The default, type 6 (which includes gridlines on the chart), will do fine.

🖱 *If necessary, select Type 6 and click* `Next >`*. (You could double-click Type 6 instead.)*

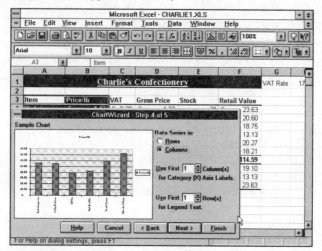

This is first preview of what your chart will look like. There are three options here concerning the data in the chart. The Chart Wizard makes some 'educated' guesses as to what you are likely to want and presents those as defaults.

The **Data Series** (Price/lb.) is in a column on the worksheet, so the first option, Data Series in: should be specified as Columns.

✍ *A data series is a collection of values taken from cells in a worksheet. These values are the points that Excel plots in its charts.*

🖱 *Ensure that the Data Series in: option is specified as Columns.*

The first column of the selected range in the worksheet contains the sweet names. These should be used as labels for the data (the sweet prices). Therefore, the first column should be set to act as the category labels on the X (horizontal) axis.

🖱 *Ensure that this is set.*

The **Legend** is the box currently displayed at the right of the Sample Chart box. It identifies the data series to the reader, in this case, 'Price/lb.'. Legends can be very useful, particularly in charts containing more than one series. Notice that the text 'Price/lb.' has been used as a default title for the chart.

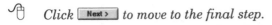 *Click* Next > *to move to the final step.*

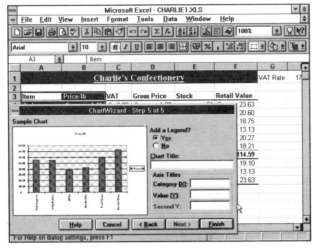

In this step, you can specify whether or not you want a legend (by default, one would be added). Here, there is only one data series (the sweet prices) and there is no need to differentiate this from any other series. A legend would be useful if, for example, you wanted to show the Cost/lb. for this year and last year, for each item.

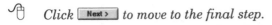 *Click the No option button so that no legend is placed on the chart.*

Below the legend section, there is a series of boxes allowing you to add titles to go on the chart. You can move from box to box either by clicking in them or by using Tab to move down and Shift Tab to move up.

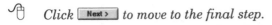 *Move to the Chart Title box and type* Sweet Prices

Note that the title appears in the middle at the top of the chart preview window, replacing the default title. Titles on charts have certain default positions, bound to whichever element of the chart they are labelling, e.g. the Category (X) Axis Title will be fixed in a certain position in relation to the horizontal X Axis.

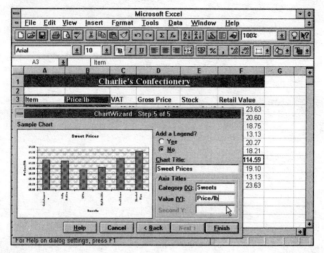

Move to the 'Category (X)' text box and type Sweets *as the title then move to the 'Value (Y)' text box and type* Price/lb. *into that box.*

The chart is now designed, and you are ready to insert it into the workbook.

Click Finish *to create the chart.*

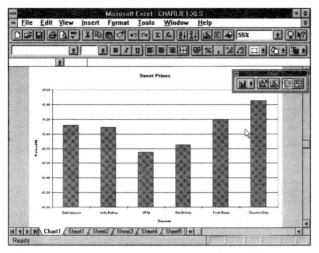

A new sheet with the default name 'Chart1' has appeared to display the chart. When Excel created the chart, a new toolbar also appeared – the Chart toolbar.

——————— Changing the chart ———————

This column chart is excellent for viewing the comparative costs per pound of the sweets that Charlie stocks. You may also be interested in seeing it in a different way. The Chart Wizard could be used again to create a new chart in, say, Doughnut style, but this isn't necessary. The Chart toolbar allows you to change the current chart type, applying a new type to the same data.

🖑 *Click the drop-down button on the Chart Type tool* 📊 *to see the palette of chart types.*

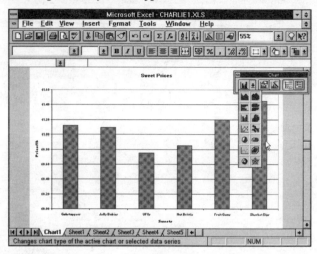

🖑 *Select the 3-D Pie chart type (fifth down on the right).*

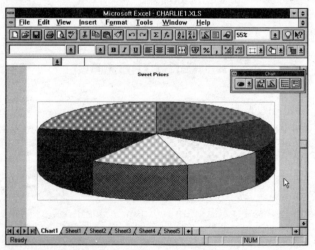

The labels which identified the sweets have disappeared. These labels are still available, and would be displayed again if you switched back to the Column chart. By default they are not used on pie charts.

Adding a legend

It would be useful to see a legend here, as you no longer have
category labels for the sweet types. The Legend tool  on the
Chart toolbar can be used to display a legend box showing the
names of the different sweet types and the colours (and patterns) used for the associated pie sections.

🖰   *Click the Legend tool*  *on the Chart toolbar.*

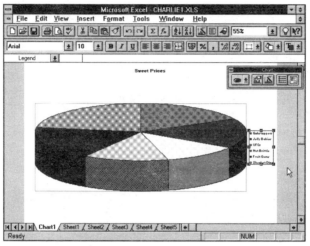

The button remains depressed, showing that a legend has been
applied to this chart. The legend could be removed by clicking
the legend button again.

Highlighting a segment

It is possible to highlight individual segments of a pie chart, so
as to apply formatting to that particular part of the chart. With
pie (and doughnut) charts, it is even possible to remove a segment from its position on the pie. This is done by selecting it
and then dragging it away from the pie.

🖱 *Click the pie chart once to select it.*

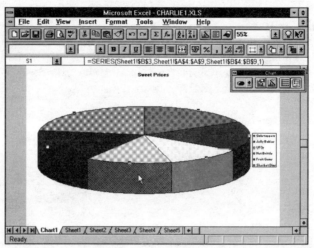

This first click selects the whole chart. Note the handles around the chart.

🖱 *Click again on any segment.*

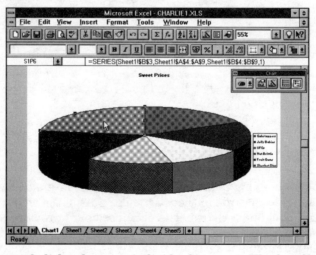

The second click selects an individual segment The handles are now around the selected segment only. The first and second clicks must be clearly separate – a double-click will open the

Format Data Series dialog. Now that you have selected the segment, you can manipulate it separately.

 Drag the segment away from the centre.

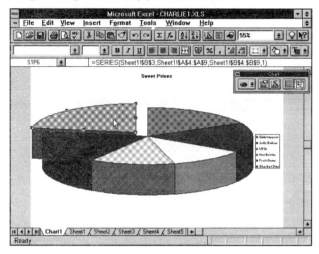

To put the segment back into the main pie, it is tempting to try to reposition it exactly where it came from. This often leads to small gaps at either side of the slice. To ensure that the segment will rejoin the pie, flush at either end, drag it back towards the centre of the pie until it will go no further. This ensures that the slice will be repositioned properly in the pie.

🖰 *Reform the pie by trying to drag the slice back through the centre.*

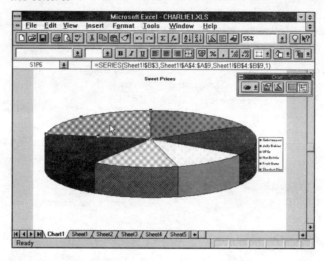

——The Chart Wizard tool——

🖰 *Switch back to Sheet1 of the workbook (click its tab).*

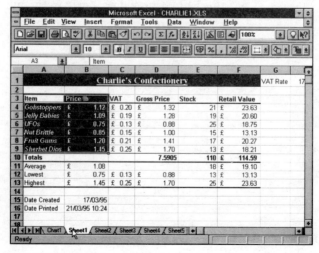

The previous section showed that a chart can be produced by clicking with the right mouse button on a sheet tab and choosing Insert, then specifying Chart. This is one way of producing a chart. It is also possible to **embed** a chart in the worksheet. This means that it would appear in the worksheet itself rather than on a sheet in its own right.

The Chart Wizard tool 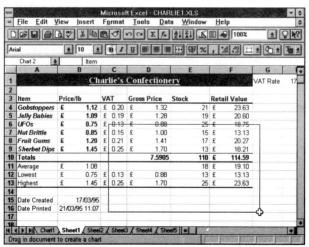 on the Standard toolbar will activate the Chart Wizard dialog to produce a chart embedded in the current worksheet.

Make sure cells A3:B9 are selected. Click on the toolbar.

If you move the mouse pointer over the worksheet (don't drag yet), you will see that the pointer shape has changed. The message bar indicates that Excel expects you to drag out an area for the chart. The chart can be embedded in any area of the sheet, though should it overlap any data, it will not overwrite it. The chart is an **object**, and can be thought of as floating *on top of* the cells. Furthermore, the area that you select can be moved and sized later, if necessary.

Drag out an area for the chart.

If you drag close to the edges of the worksheet, you will find that Excel scrolls to allow you to select a bigger area. Don't worry if this happens: simply drag to the opposite edge to make the worksheet scroll back again. The important thing is not to let go of the mouse button until you are sure that the area is the size that you want.

After a short delay, the Chart Wizard starts and the dialog for step one is presented.

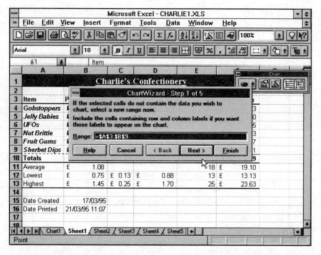

Click Finish *to accept all the default options and create the chart.*

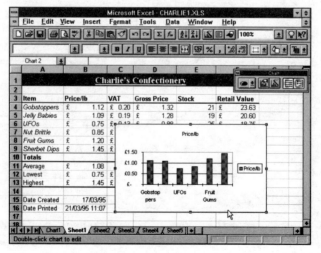

Don't be concerned that the chart currently covers some of your data. You will shortly see how to move it to any desired position on the sheet.

Re-sizing an embedded chart

When an embedded chart is selected, handles appear on it, along the edges and at the corners. These can be dragged to re-size the chart.

 Practise re-sizing the chart.

Deleting an embedded chart

To delete an embedded chart, first make sure it is selected. A selected chart has re-sizing handles visible. Then, press Del.

Formatting charts

Whichever type of chart you have created – whether on a new chart sheet or embedded in the worksheet – you can format the components of the chart in various ways.

In order to edit an embedded chart you must first activate its edit mode. This can be done by double-clicking it, or by selecting it and choosing Edit Object

🖰 *Double-click the embedded chart.*

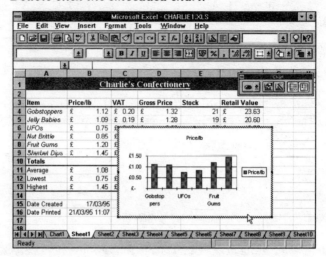

The shaded line around the chart indicates that you are currently editing the object. If the embedded chart had been too big to fit in the Excel window, you would have been presented with the whole chart in a new window. The title bar of that window would have given the workbook and sheet names as well as the name of the chart.

You can edit the chart in the same way whether you see it inside the shaded border or inside its own window. The difference comes when you finish editing. With a shaded border, you can click any cell on the worksheet to go back to editing that. When the chart is within a window, you have to close the window itself, for example, using its document control menu.

Editing a chart sheet is even easier – you do not have to double-click the chart; you can immediately edit the chart.

You will notice that during editing, the menu bar has changed: some of the normal menus are not appropriate for chart editing, so are not presented.

A general principle of chart formatting is 'double-click the item that you want to format'. For example, suppose that you want to change the colours or shading of the data columns:

Double-click one of the data columns.

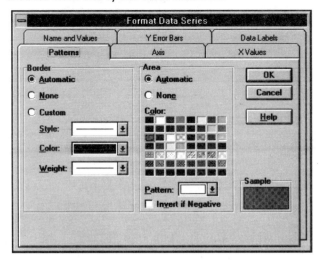

The resulting dialog is the 'Format Data Series' dialog. The Patterns tab is of particular interest here.

 Choose the Patterns tab, if it is not already selected.

Pick a colour from the palette in the Area section and click OK .

The series of data columns changes colour. All chart components can be formatted by the same method: double-click the component in which you are interested. A format dialog will appear, appropriate to the element being edited.

 Try formatting another part of the chart, for example the legend or the background.

If you need to insert new chart components, for example titles, the quickest method is to right-click the chart: this will give a shortcut menu from which you can choose the appropriate option. Alternatively, you can use the Insert menu.

For example, you could insert some axis titles:

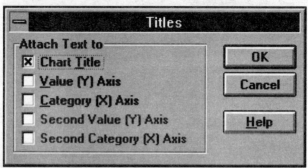

Right-click the area of the chart outside the axes and choose Insert Titles from the shortcut menu.

The dialog allows insertion of chart and axis titles.

Check the ⊠ Value (Y) Axis, and ⊠ Category (X) Axis and click ___OK___

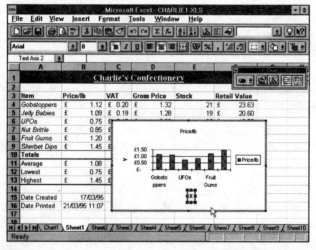

X and Y axis titles have been inserted with default text. To replace these defaults, select the appropriate title and type the new text. If you want to edit an existing title, select it and then click it again. You will then be able to edit that title.

*Change the X and Y titles to **Sweets** and **Price** respectively. When you've finished editing a title, press [Esc]*

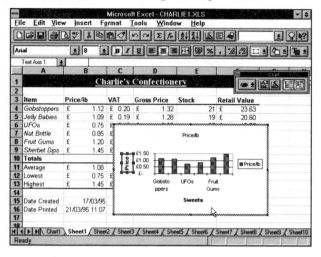

Moving an embedded chart

An embedded chart can be moved using drag-and-drop. Earlier, you saw how to move a block of cells by picking it up with the mouse pointer and dragging it across the sheet. Since the chart currently obscures part of the table, it would be useful to move it to a different part of the worksheet.

🖰 *Press* ⌨ *to deactivate the chart (but note it still has handles and is selected). Position the mouse pointer anywhere over the chart. Click and hold to select the chart. Then drag the grey outline until it is in the required position.*

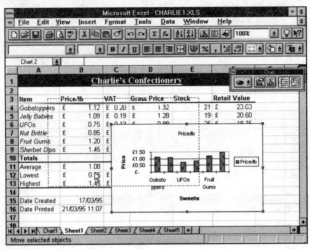

You will notice that if you drag the chart off the edge of the display, the screen scrolls to follow your movement.

🖰 *Let go of the mouse button and scroll if necessary to see the entire chart.*

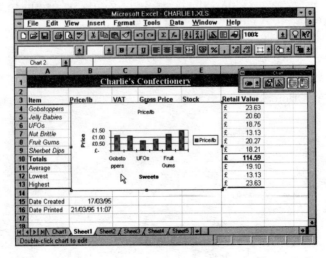

A similar technique can be used to move an embedded chart, even if the chart is being edited (and has a shaded border). In that case, the white arrow pointer must be pointing at the striped edge of the chart before clicking to select it. An embedded chart cannot be moved on the sheet if it is being edited in a separate window as happens, for example, when it is too large to be fully displayed on the screen.

 Click a cell on the worksheet (or close the chart editing window via the document control menu) to deselect the chart.

Embedded charts are deleted by selecting them and pressing ☐Del☐. Alternatively, you can right-click over them and choose Clear.

 Do this now.

Summary: Charting
- Charts are easily produced by using the Chart Wizard.
- The Chart Wizard guides you through the process in five steps.
- Previews are given in the final stages.
- Charts can be embedded in a worksheet or be a separate chart sheet.
- Embedded charts can be re-sized using their selection handles and moved by dragging and dropping.

12

—— TIPS AND HELP ——

This chapter covers:
- ToolTips.
- The TipWizard.
- The Help system.

——————ToolTips——————

ToolTips were introduced in an earlier chapter: they are the little yellow tags that appear when you position your mouse pointer over a toolbar button and hover. They give an indication of the function of that button. You may not have noticed that whenever a ToolTip is displayed you will also find a fuller explanation on the status bar.

The TipWizard

The TipWizard aims to give help as you work about the way you work. It gives tips about alternative, and often quicker, ways of performing actions as you perform them or useful information about current work.

🖰 *Click 💡 on the standard toolbar.*

The TipWizard appears as a toolbar.

You will notice that the box contains a useful tip about one of the activities you recently performed in Excel. At the right edge of the box there is a pair of **spinners** 🔼. These can be used to view previous tips. Even though you have not been displaying the TipWizard, you will find that it has still been coming up with suggestions for actions as you performed them. These tips have been stored in case you wish to look at them later.

🖰 *Use the spinners to see other useful tips, all of which will be relevant to what you have been doing.*

If you want to know more about a tip, click 💡 which will launch the Help system. Notice 💡 is now white – when there is a new tip, it will turn yellow again. When you have finished browsing tips, you can turn its display off by clicking 💡. You would only do this if you did not wish to leave the TipWizard active for more tips as you work.

🖰 *Click 💡 to close the TipWizard.*

The Help tool

Earlier, you used the Chart Wizard. If you wanted to know more about the Chart Wizard, you could look in the User Guide, which will certainly have some information on the subject. But the User Guide may not be to hand, and even if it is, it often refers the user to the on-line Help system. You can access the Help system via the Help menu, but allows you to activate help by clicking items on the screen that are of interest to you. The Help application will then open to show information relevant to what you clicked.

Click

Your mouse pointer takes on a new shape: ?.

Try clicking something you want to know more about, for example the Chart Wizard tool

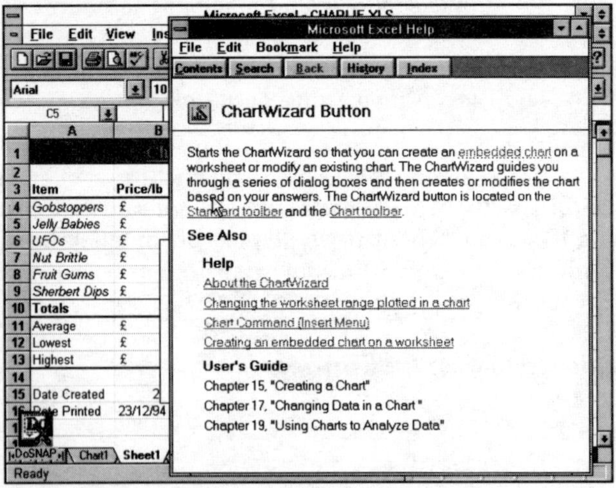

Help is a separate application from Excel. The Help window opens here, with Excel still visible behind. The size of the Help window will vary, and it may not be the above size on your machine.

It is not necessary to close Help entirely before trying out the things you have read in Help. You can use ⟨Alt⟩⟨Tab⟩ to cycle through each of the open applications.

The Help pointer can be used in a similar way to show information about a menu item. It can be cancelled by typing ⟨Esc⟩ or clicking ↘? again.

Using Help

Help buttons

When you activate the help system and the help window is displayed, you will find a row of buttons at the top of the window. These can be used to navigate you through the pages of help.

Contents	Takes you to the Contents page of Help.
Search	Searches for keywords or topics specified by the user.
Back	Backtracks one-by-one through the pages of Help that you have viewed so far in this session.
History	Gives you a list of the topics that you have looked at allowing you to return to them.
Index	Takes you to the Index page of Help.

Glossaries and cross-references

If you position the mouse pointer over a green underlined word or phrase, the pointer turns into a hand.

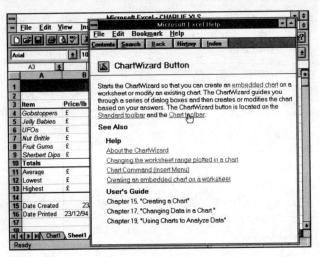

This indicates that clicking that word or phrase will take the user to further information related to it. A dotted underline indicates an item that has a glossary entry.

🖑 *Click* <u>embedded chart</u> *to see its Glossary entry.*

To put the box away:

🖑 *Click the Glossary entry box.*

A solid, green underline indicates a cross-referenced item – clicking this allows you to find out more about the item concerned.

Click <u>About the ChartWizard</u>

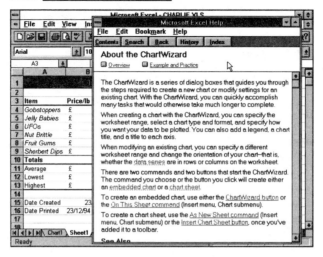

The Overview button would take you to a page of general information about the topic. The Example and Practice button would take you to an example and interactive practice session concerned with the topic.

Back

Clicking **Back** will take you back to a previously viewed page.

 *Click* **Back** .

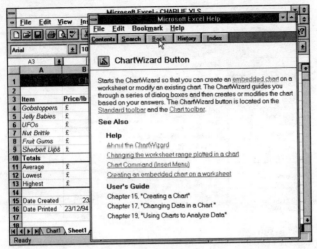

Search

You might want to search for help on a particular word or phrase. The Search command offers a list of terms or descriptions on which help is available.

⌐ Click **Search**

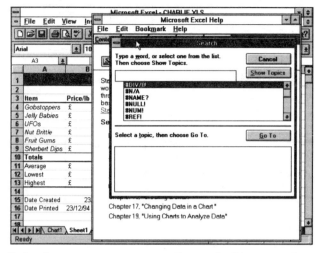

This dialog has two stages to it. First of all, a topic has to be chosen from the top half of the dialog. You can either scroll down the list of topics or type what you hope to know more about.

⌐ Type **chart legends**, *watching the screen as you do so.*

Notice as you type each letter that Excel 'closes in' on the text. You don't actually need to type all of the word **legends**: Excel will have chosen this topic as soon as you've typed enough of the word to distinguish it from other help topics on charts.

 *Click* Show Topics .

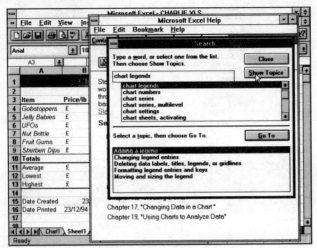

Several topics relating to chart legends are offered for selection in the lower window.

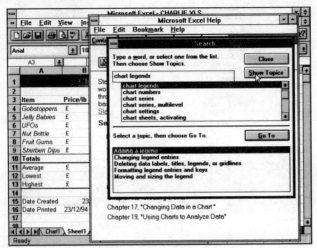 *Select the 'Adding a legend' topic and click* Go To

How to

A How To window appears with step-by-step instructions on adding a legend.

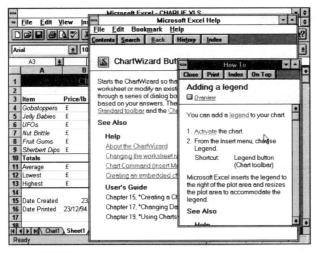

If you click  **On Top** and then click the workbook, the instructions would stay displayed on top of the Excel window allowing you to follow them as you carry them out. Clearly, you may need to move the Help window around to keep your work visible. For now, close the How To window:

🖑 *Click* **Close**

Contents

✍ *To return to the Contents page of Help, click* Contents

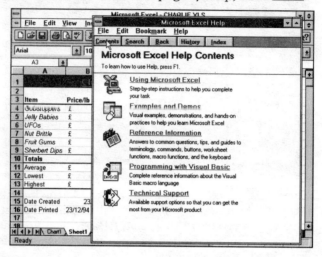

History

✍ *Click* History

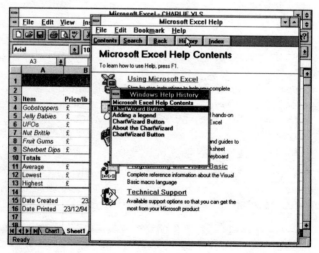

The History window shows you all the pages you have looked at in this Help session. Pages may be shown more than once, indicating that you have looked at those pages more than once. You could double-click any of these to jump back to the relevant page.

✍ *Double-click 'Chart Wizard Button' in the History window.*

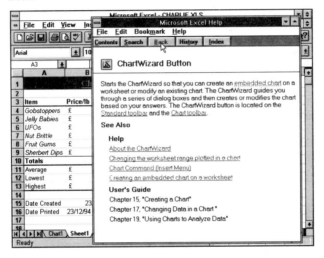

Index

The Index is an alphabetical list of topics for which Help is available.

You can browse the Index and click any of the entries to display a page of Help relevant to the subject. Some of the references are arranged under headings, with indented sub-entries. Clicking the heading will not do anything, but the sub-entries can be activated by clicking them.

You can browse the list by using the scroll bar or click one of the letter buttons at the top of the window to move to the first of the entries for that letter in the Index.

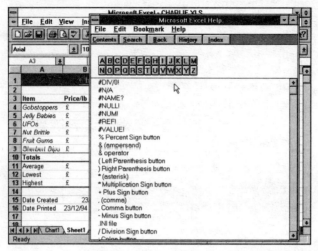

Leaving Help

You can leave Help by several means: for example, by selecting File Exit, selecting the Control Menu 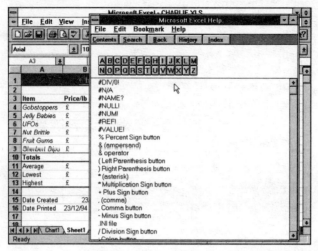 for Help and then selecting Close, double-clicking, or pressing [Alt] [F4]

Use one of these methods to exit the Help application.

Close the current workbook, using File Close.

If you try to close a file that has been changed since it was last saved, Excel will ask you if you want to save it as you close it.

Summary: Tips and Help

- The TipWizard gives helpful information about the way you work, as you work.

- Clicking 🔃 and then clicking on an item on the screen will give you Help information on the item that you selected.

- Green highlighted words or phrases with dotted underlining have glossary entries defined for them. They can be accessed by clicking on them.

- Green highlighted words or phrases with solid underlining indicate a cross-reference to another topic, which can again be accessed by clicking on the word.

- Specific topics can be found using the Search facility.

- 'How To' gives you step-by-step instructions on completing various tasks. These instructions can be left on screen to follow as you work.

- The Index can also be browsed to select relevant topics.

13

MANIPULATING THE WORKSHEET

This chapter covers:
- Entering sequences using the Fill handle.
- The difference between clearing and deleting cells, rows and columns.
- The problems created with formulae when moving rows or columns.
- Sorting rows and columns alphabetically.

———— A few experiments ————

By this stage, you will probably be comfortable with the idea of typing data and formulae into cells and copying those formulae (via the Fill handle or by other methods) to build up your spreadsheet. Excel provides a wealth of features concerned with making spreadsheet design quick and easy. This section begins by performing a few experiments to introduce and explore some of Excel's features.

Using AutoFill to enter sequential data

The first technique to examine involves the use of the Fill handle. You will have seen some of the capabilities of the Fill handle already in the form of a quick and easy method of copying and pasting cell contents. The following exercise will explore the Fill handle's capabilities more fully.

The behaviour of the Fill handle is quite interesting. It is capable of recognising and extending series based on, amongst others, numbers, dates, ordinal numbers (1st, 2nd, 3rd, etc.) and day names.

A new workbook would be useful in this example. If there are no blank workbooks currently displayed, click □ to display one. (The book in our example is named 'Book3', but yours may have a different number). Make sure a blank workbook is the active document, type **Quarter 1** *in cell A1 and then press* Enter

Select cell A1 and drag the Fill handle across to column D.

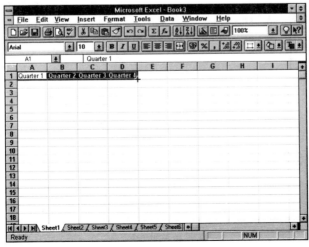

The series is extended.

🖱 *Now drag the Fill handle further along the row to column I.*

As you might have predicted, the series is extended again. Note that as once you have reached Quarter 4, the series starts again at Quarter 1.

The next four examples demonstrate the extension of a linear series: in this case, you must select the first two values in the series to specify the interval for the series.

🖱 *In cell A2 type 1 and in cell B2 type 2*

🖱 *Select the cells A2:B2 and drag the Fill handle across to column D.*

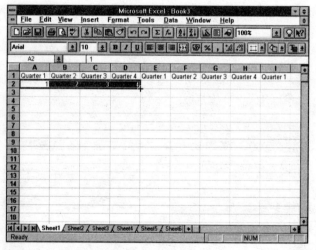

The specified series, in this case incrementing by 1, is extended. Excel will also treat ordinal numbers correctly.

You can use the Fill handle to extend more than one cell at once.

Type **1st Batch** *in A5,* **2nd Batch** *in B5,* **3rd Batch** *in A6 and* **5th Batch** *in B6.*

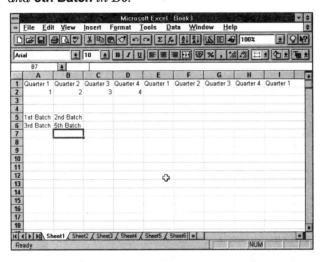

Select A5:B5 and drag the Fill handle to column F.

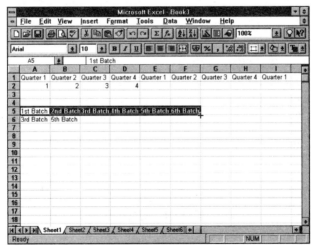

You can always extend the series further by dragging the Fill handle again.

🖱 *Drag the Fill handle to column I.*

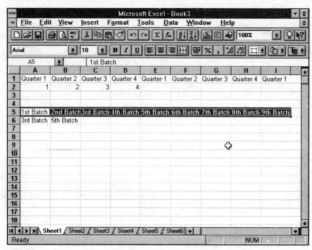

🖱 *Select A6:B6 and drag the Fill handle across to column I*

You can use the Fill handle to fill a series in two dimensions as well.

🖱 *Select A5:I6 and extend the series in each of the columns by dragging the Fill handle down to row 10.*

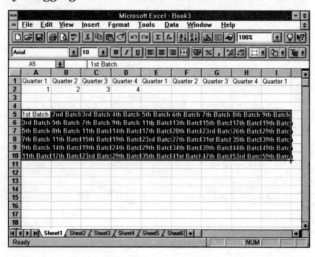

Generally, you can extend several numeric series (i.e. ones with more than one initial value) at once. Because you were extending the series in a vertical direction, Excel interpreted each column of data separately: the values in column A increase by 2 each time; in column B, they increase by 3 each time, and so forth.

Text and date series can only be extended individually. However, a group of text or date values can be extended together:

 In A12, type **01-Jan**. *In A13, type* **26/02/95**.

In A14, type **Jan**. *In A15, type* **Mon**.

Select A12 to A15 in turn and use the Fill handle to create series based on each of these dates.

Notice that the last two are simply text, but Excel recognises them as being significant as dates.

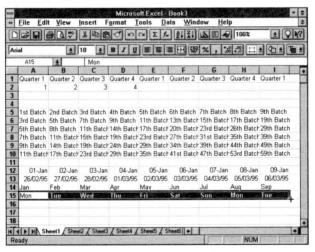

AutoFill can be used to create vertical series in the same way.

& *Excel will extend numeric series of three or more initial values along a best-fit straight line by linear regression.*

—— Creating a custom AutoFill list ——

You can also create a custom list for a sequence of words that you frequently type, e.g. the products you sell or the names of your staff. Custom AutoFill lists, once created, are available in any worksheet.

🖰 *Click a blank cell so that no text is selected. From the Tools menu select Options... and click the Custom Lists dialog tab.*

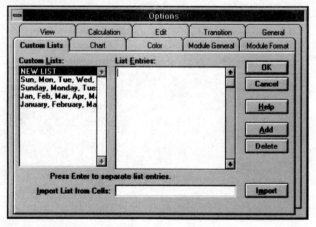

🖰 *Choose NEW LIST from Custom Lists. Type the entries for a list (you could use our example below) in the List Entries box, separating each entry by pressing* Enter*.*

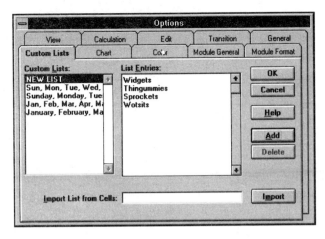

🖑 *Click* **Add** *to add the new list and* **OK** *to exit the dialog.*

Now, try to use this custom list.

🖑 *Select the cell A17 and type in any of the names from your list. Use the Fill handle to fill the custom list horizontally into the next few cells.*

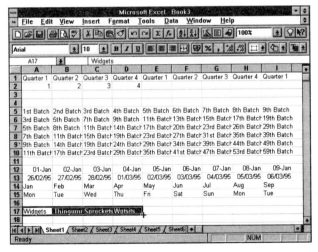

👍 *Note that what will be entered into each cell appears in the Name box as you extend the series. This is true when using AutoFill to fill any list or series.*

You can also drag the Fill handle left or upwards to create decreasing series. The Fill handle behaves exactly as when dragged down or to the right, but creates the series in reverse.

🖰 *Select cell I18, type 'September' and drag the Fill handle backwards to cell A18.*

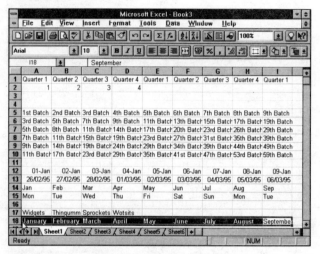

Copying formats using AutoFill

The Fill handle will not only fill adjacent cells with data, but can also be used to copy formats. Imagine a partially complete spreadsheet, with some cells formatted and others not. Suppose that you simply wish to extend the formats of these cells to encompass the new cells. You could use 🖋, but another way is to use the Fill handle, but this time dragging with the right mouse button.

🖰 *Click cell A14 and format Jan so that it appears in italics.*

Dragging with the left mouse button will simply overwrite any existing cell contents, but using the right mouse button will give you a range of choices about how you wish to drag out the cell, one of which is to fill only formats, not cell contents.

Make sure that the active cell is A12. Click the Fill handle with the right mouse button and drag to column I.

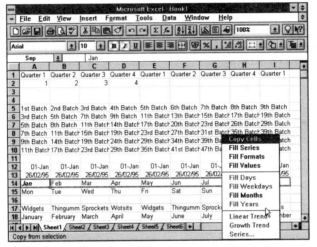

The shortcut menu that appears depends on the original selection. Since you had only one cell selected to start with, series options do not apply. In this case, you wish to copy the formats only.

🖱 *Choose Fill Formats.*

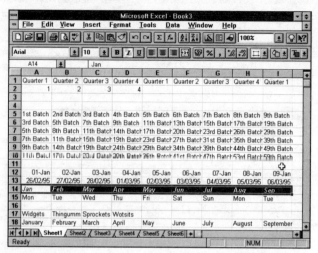

🖱 *In cell F2, type £12. Click with the right mouse button and drag to cell I2. Choose Fill Formats.*

This applies currency formatting to G2:I2.

🖱 *Enter 10 in cell G2.*

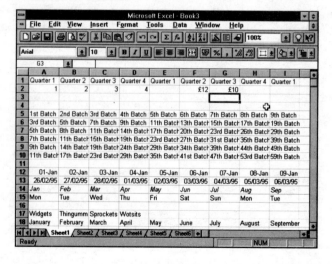

Since currency formatting has already been applied to cell G2, its contents appear as £10.

The cell inherits the number format of its dependent cells. Excel will assume that cells calculated from other cells that all have the same format also require that format.

The Fill handle shortcut menu can also be used to fill a series in different ways: for example, perhaps you want a list of weekdays rather than all the days of the week.

Choose a blank sheet, type **Monday** *in cell A1 and extend the series down to cell A15 by dragging the Fill handle using the right mouse button. Choose Fill Weekdays from the shortcut menu.*

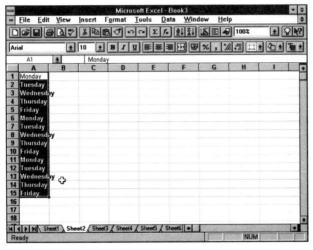

The extended series of days does not now include the weekend.

Deleting and clearing cells

There are many ways of removing the contents of a cell, some of which you may already have used (Edit Clear All for example). Some of the other convenient methods are as follows:

The delete key

You can delete cell contents very easily by using ⌜Del⌟.

⌂ *Select the cell on the sheet containing the first* **Wednesday** *and press* ⌜Del⌟

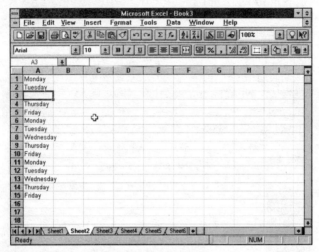

⌜Del⌟ is equivalent to Edit Clear Contents.

> ✍ *Users of version 4 of the product will recognise this as the action of* ⌜Ctrl⌟ ⌜Del⌟. *It should be noted that* ⌜Ctrl⌟ ⌜Del⌟ *in version 5 still functions in the same way, for the purpose of backward compatibility.*

⌂ *Undo the clear using* 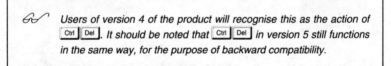 *so that you can try another method.*

Fill handle clearing

The Fill handle can be used to clear cells by dragging back into the selection.

⌂ *Select all the days of the second week.*

Drag the Fill handle back to the Monday of the second week.

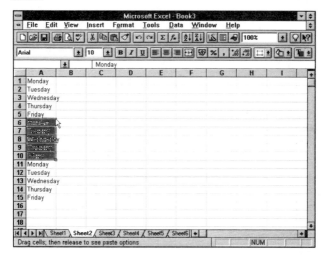

As you drag the cells become grey; when you let go, the values (but not the formats) will be cleared.

 Undo again.

Deleting cells

Clearing the cells removes the unwanted information but leaves a gap in the sheet. Suppose you now want to close the gap and make the table tidier. You could do this by first clearing the cells and then copying the information from one area to another, but there is a quicker method. You can remove certain cells entirely by deleting (as opposed to clearing) them.

Select Thursday and Friday of the first week and choose Edit Delete.

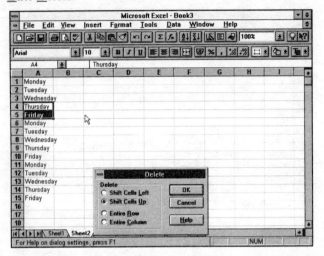

The dialog gives the option of removing the entire row or column. In general, it is a good idea not to be too cavalier with deleting entire rows or columns in worksheets, especially if you are unsure of the underlying structure of the workbook. The remaining options will delete just the selected cells. Excel needs to know which way to shift the rest of the sheet in order to 'plug' the gap. It should be clear in this case that the cells should shift up.

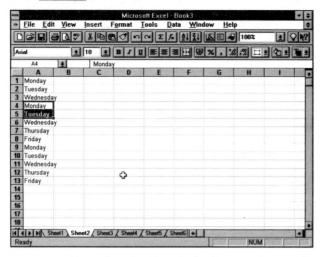

Click ⦿ *Shift Cells Up, if it is not already selected, then click* OK

There are no options for clearing formats or values only when you are deleting as the cells themselves are removed. Undo is still available however. You may like to note that `Ctrl` `-` is the keyboard shortcut for Edit Delete.

Earlier, you saw how to add extra rows to a spreadsheet. The method for deleting rows or columns is similar: highlight the row or column using its heading, then either choose Edit Delete, or right-click the heading and choose Delete.

🖑 *Enter* **Marker** *into cell B1.*

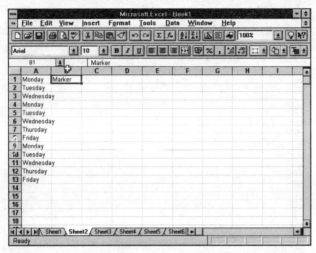

🖑 *Delete column A (for example, by clicking its grey column heading to select the column and then using Edit Delete).*

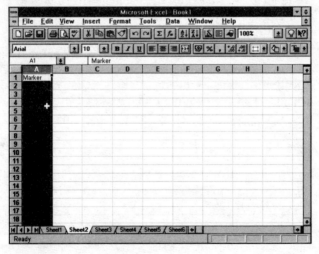

🖑 *Use* 🔄 *to undo the deletion.*

Moving rows using drag and drop

Sometimes it is desirable to move rows to new locations. A variation of the drag and drop technique is particularly useful here.

 Type England, Wales, Scotland *and* Ireland *in cells C13:C16. Type the numbers* 1, 2, 3, 4 *beside each entry in column D.*

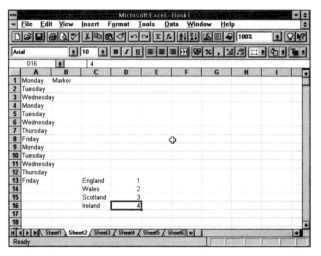

Suppose that you want to move the Wales data below the Scotland data. You could insert some cells and then shuffle everything around but that would be a bit cumbersome.

 Select the 'Wales' cells, C14:D14. Place the mouse pointer on the edge of the selection area and begin to drag. Keep the mouse button held down.

Up to this point, things should be familiar – you are using drag and drop to move the row. However, the usual drag and drop will replace the contents of the target cells (after a warning) which is not what you want to do in this case. Drag and drop can be made to insert cells rather than to overwrite the target cells.

 Hold down Shift, *while keeping the mouse button held down.*

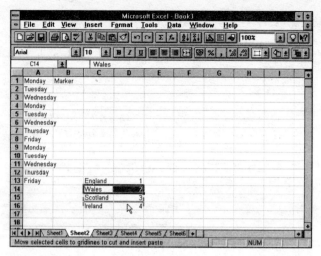

Notice that the grey outline changes to an insertion bar. This moves so as to lie along the edge of the cells, indicating where the selected cell will be inserted. Warning: be sure that the insertion bar is lying along the correct horizontal or vertical edge before releasing the mouse button!

Hold down the mouse button until the insertion bar is between rows 15 and 16. Then release the mouse button and then release Shift*.*

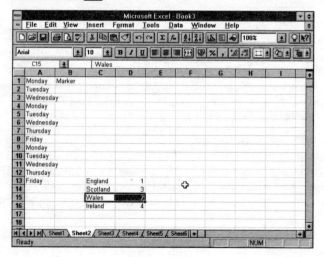

Make sure you release the mouse button before the [Shift] key, otherwise you will perform a normal drag and drop. Technically, the [Shift] key needs be held down only as you release the mouse button.

Moving rows – care with formulae

Care is always needed whenever rows and columns are deleted or inserted, but special consideration should be given to the effect on formulae.

✍ *Open* `C:\EXCEL5\EXCELCBT\ART.XLS` *and click the Music tab.*

This file is one of those provided when you install Excel. If you haven't got these files you may need to reinstall part of Excel – see appendix B.

✍ *Type new items in cells A8 to E8:* **Apr, 800, 1200, 930,240** *and copy the formula in column F down to this row.*

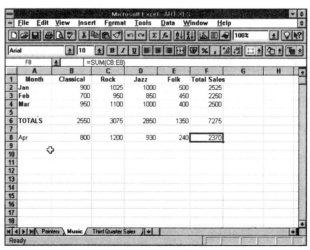

Suppose you take this row and insert it in between rows 4 and 5 in the list above:

Select the new data and use Shift *with drag and drop to insert the data between rows 4 and 5.*

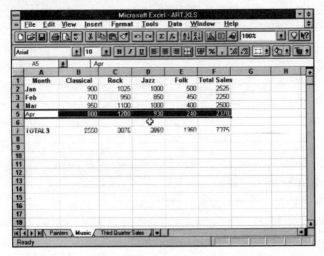

Check the Totals figure in cell B7 then click in the cell to examine the formula.

With the figures for April now included in the table, you might reasonably have expected Excel to update the TOTALS row. A check on the TOTALS indicates that this has not happened. The reason for this occurring lies in the SUM formula. Although the April figures are now in the table, they are still outside the range in the SUM formula used to determine the TOTALS. To obtain the correct TOTALS, you have to extend the range in the SUM formula to include the newly inserted row. Care should therefore be taken when inserting new rows into a table to include them, where necessary, in the range of any formulas used.

Make sure cell B7 is selected and click Σ

Fill this revised formula across to the other totals in this row.

——— Sorting rows and columns ———

Excel provides easy to use features to sort tables of data.

🖱 *Open the file* C:\EXCEL5\EXCELCBT\93SALES.XLS *from the* EXCELCBT *directory.*

🖱 *Use the tab scrolling buttons* 🔲◀▶🔲 *to find the tab for the Products sheet, then click it.*

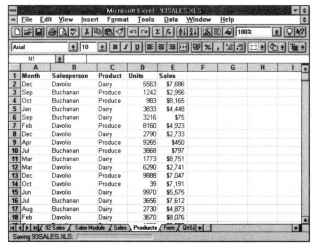

This table lists the sales in different areas for the company's sales personnel. Suppose you want to sort this list of data based upon the name of the salesperson.

The sort tools

🔼 and 🔽 on the standard toolbar provide a quick means to sort selections into ascending and descending order respectively. If no range is selected, the column containing the active cell will be used for the **key** – that is, the values on which the table will be sorted. Since you want the salesperson to be the key, you should ensure that the active cell is somewhere in the salesperson column. If no range has been selected, Excel will choose a range for you, as seen earlier. Here, if no range is selected, Excel will choose the entire block of data

🖰 *Select a cell in the Salesperson column (B) and click* 🔽

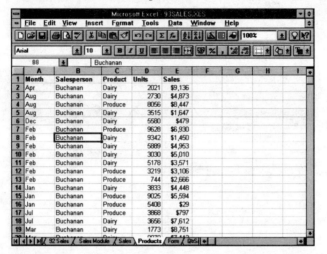

🖰 *Try* 🔼

Excel always sorts by rows if the sort tools are used. If you wanted to sort the columns into alphabetical order you would have to use another method involving the sort dialog. The tools on the toolbar represent ascending and descending order, and can be used to sort not only alphabetical characters, but numerical characters as well.

🖰 *Try sorting the Sales or Units columns using the tools.*

Notice that Excel somehow recognises that Salesperson is a heading, not a name and excludes row 1 in the sort. You might assume that Excel has guessed that the first row is always the heading row, but it is much more clever than that. It has noticed that the word Salesperson is in a different format and has assumed that it is therefore a heading.

The Sort dialog

The Sort dialog provides more control over the way in which Excel performs sorting.

 *Ensure that the active cell is within the data block and select Data Sort...*

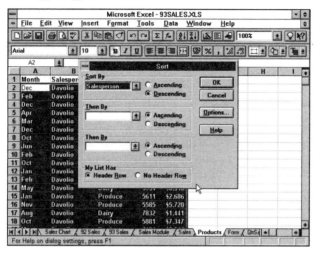

Note that you can say whether your data includes a header.

 *Click* **Options...** .

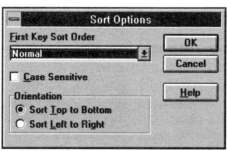

From this dialog, you can control the details of how a sort will be carried out. Sorts may be case sensitive, in which upper case letters are placed before lower case. Special sort orders may be defined to place certain words in other than alphabetic order (days of the week, months of the year etc.: pull down the list to see some examples). Also, the orientation of the sort can be set: in this case, sort left to right produces our desired result.

🖱 *Click ● Sort Left to Right*

🖱 *Click* [OK] *to return to the Sort dialog.*

Now, the key row can be supplied. Up to three keys can be defined in the sort dialog. The second key is used in the event of two or more rows/columns containing identical values for the first key; the third key is used if the first and second keys produce a tie.

🖱 *Ensure that the Sort By field shows 'Row 1' then click* [OK] *to sort the columns.*

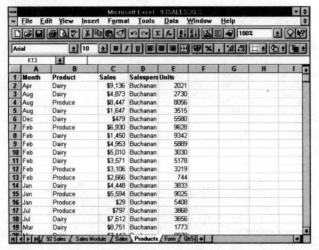

Clearly the column widths are a little confused: although the columns have swapped position, the column width formatting applied to them has been left where it was. To best-fit all the columns in the table:

Click the select all button ☐ (to the left of column A and above row 1) and double-click between any of the column headings.

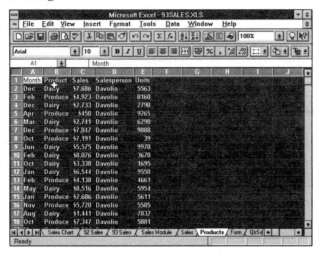

Summary: Manipulating the worksheet

- The workbook can be saved by clicking ▣.
- AutoFill can be used to enter sequences of various types. Dragging the Fill handle with the right mouse button results in a shortcut menu giving further options.
- Custom lists for use with the Fill handle can be added using Tools Options Custom Lists.
- Cells are deleted using the Delete option from the Edit or Shortcut menus.
- Del **clears** cell contents. It does not remove formatting and it does not delete the cell.
- The Fill handle can be used to clear a cell range by dragging inside the cell range and releasing.
- Moving, deleting and inserting rows may affect formulae and other parts of the worksheet – care must be taken.
- Columns and rows can be rearranged using the mouse.
- Rows and Columns can be sorted alphabetically (also numerically etc.) using either ⬛ and ⬛ for a quick sort or the Sort option on the Data menu for more detailed control.

14

WORKBOOK MANIPULATION

This chapter covers:

- Renaming worksheets.
- Copying the contents of a whole worksheet to another worksheet.
- Selecting several worksheets and editing them as a group.
- Copying across worksheets.
- Working with 3-D formulae.

Excel provides a 16-sheet workbook by default. So far, the spreadsheets you have created have dealt only with separate, unconnected sheets. This chapter explores some of Excel's workbook capabilities.

Renaming a worksheet

It is possible to give your worksheet a name other than the default Sheet1, Sheet2, etc. You can give a sheet a name up to 31 characters long, including spaces. To rename the sheet you can double-click on the sheet tab, or use the rename option on the short-cut menu.

Open the file `C:\EXCEL5\EXCELCBT\93SALES.XLS`

As you can see, the sheets in this workbook have already been named.

Double-click the tab for 1993 Sales.

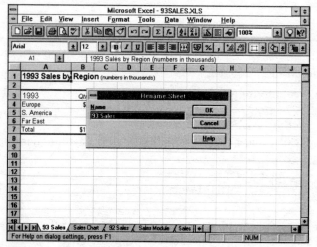

The Rename Sheet dialog appears, with the name 93 Sales displayed.

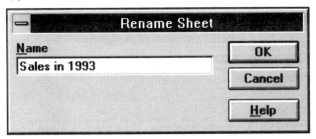

🖰 *Type in the name* **Sales in 1993**.

🖰 *Click* **OK**

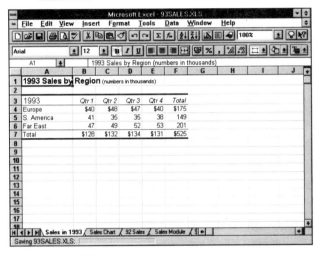

You have renamed it.

Moving a worksheet

A worksheet can be moved within a workbook using drag and drop. The Sales in 1993 sheet will be used as the basis for a set of sheets detailing sales, plus over the period 1993 to 1996 it makes sense to keep the sheets in one workbook. A quick way to generate the sheets will be to make three further copies of this Sales in 1993 sheet, one each for ...1994 ...1995 and ...1996.

🖱 *Drag the Sales in 1993 tab to the right.*

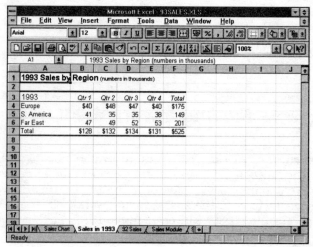

The mouse pointer now indicates that the sheet is about to be moved.

🖱 *Position the black arrow* ⬇️🔖 *between 92 Sales and Sales Module and release the mouse button.*

The Sales in 1993 tab has been moved.

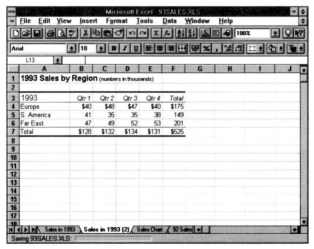 *Move the tab back to the beginning by dragging it.*

Copying a worksheet

In an earlier chapter, we saw that cells can be copied using Drag and Drop whilst holding down ⌈Ctrl⌉. Similarly, a worksheet can be copied by holding down ⌈Ctrl⌉ and dragging the worksheet tab to a new position.

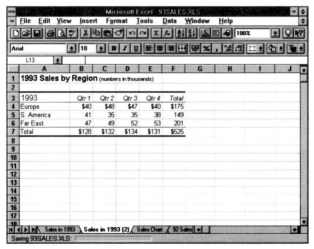 *Hold down* ⌈Ctrl⌉ *and then drag the Sales in 1993 tab so that the cursor ⍨ lies just before the Sales Chart tab.*

A copy of the Sales in 1993 sheet has been made, with the name Sales in 1993 (2). Next, you need to make two more copies and then rename them.

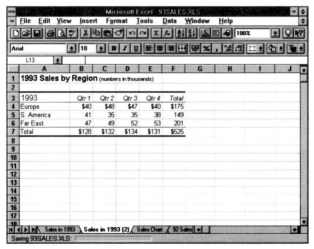 *Repeat the copy twice more so that there are four Sales in 1993 sheets altogether.*

Now you need to rename the new sheets.

🖰 *Double-click the Sales in 1993 (2) tab and name it Sales in 1994.*

🖰 *Do the same with Sales in 1993 (3) and (4) to create Sales in 1995 and Sales in 1996 tabs.*

Because the new sheets are copies, cells A1 and A3 in all of them refer to '1993 Sales by Region...' and '1993' respectively, which is inappropriate. You should edit both cells in each of the new sheets to reflect the correct year.

🖰 *Change cells A1 and A3 to show the appropriate years in each of the Sales worksheets.*

── Group editing of worksheets ──

Exercises so far have made changes to sheets individually. However, it will often be useful to make exactly the same change to a number of worksheets in a workbook. To simplify this operation, Excel provides a facility for **group editing**. Suppose the sales company in this example wanted to expand into Africa. A new row could be inserted on every sheet for

African sales. The first step in doing this is to select the group of sheets to be changed.

🖱 *Click the Sales in 1993 tab to select that sheet.*

To select several worksheets together, you can hold down `Shift` as you select other sheets.

🖱 *Hold down* `Shift` *and click the Sales in 1995 tab.*

[Group] now appears in the Title Bar to indicate that you have selected all the sheets between the first one selected and the recently chosen one – group selection is now in force. We saw earlier how you could use the select all button in the top left hand corner of the worksheet to best-fit all the column widths at once. Group editing is a similar idea, allowing you to work with many worksheets.

Worksheets can be added to an existing selection of worksheets by holding down `Ctrl` as you click. Worksheets selected in this way do not have to be sequential (although in this example Sales in 1996 is adjacent to the currently selected worksheets).

🖱 *Hold down the* `Ctrl` *key and click the Sales in 1996 tab. The 1996 sheet should now be selected in addition to the others.*

Editing as a group

To insert a new row on all of the selected sheets, it is necessary only to perform the insert operation on one of them, as long as [Group] is displayed in the title bar.

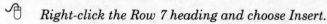 *Right-click the Row 7 heading and choose Insert.*

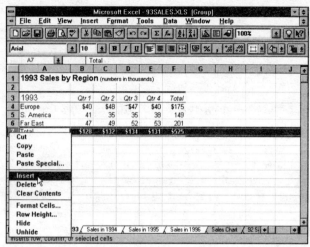

With the group still selected, anything entered into cells in one
of the selected worksheets will appear in the corresponding
cells in the others.

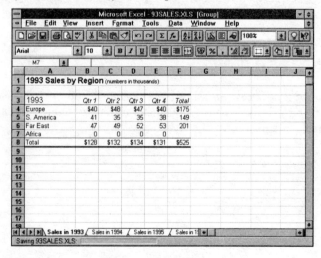 *Enter **Africa** into cell A7 and then the known sales data
of 0 into the cells for each quarter.*

Click any of the selected tabs to ensure that the group ed-
   iting has been effective, i.e. all selected tabs have been
   changed.

To deactivate a group selection, either:

• click on a tab outside the group; or

• hold down [Shift] and click the current sheet tab; or

• right-click a tab and choose Ungroup Sheets.

   Ungroup the sheets using one of the methods above.

——————— 3-D calculations ———————

Calculations can be performed using corresponding cells in selected worksheets to produce a value in one of the selection, or
in a separate sheet. This technique will be used here to perform
a five year plan calculation in a new worksheet.

First, let's set up the five year plan sheet.

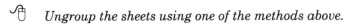   *Right-click the 1993 Sales tab and select Insert Worksheet*

   Rename it as **Five Year Plan** *and click* | **OK** |

On this sheet, net cash flow for each continent will be consoli-
dated for the five year period.

🖰 *Select cell B3 (in 'Five Year Plan') and click the AutoSum tool* Σ*.*

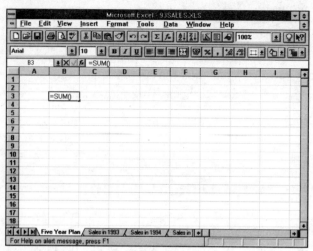

A SUM function is entered, but no cells can be found as arguments. These will be specified from the annual worksheets.

🖰 *Click the 'Sales in 1993' tab, and then cell B4*

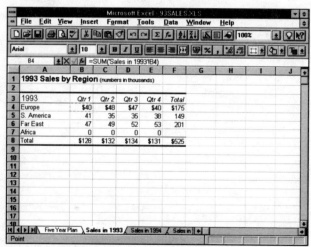

🖰 *Hold down* Shift *and click the 'Sales in 1996' tab.*

All the annual worksheets are selected. Notice that the formula
is being expanded in the formula bar.

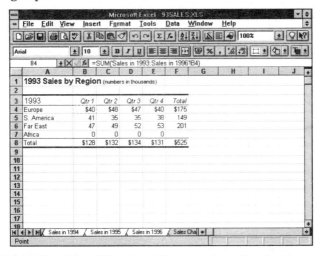

Cell B3 in Five Year Plan is still selected as the destination for
the SUM calculation. You have selected B4 in all the sheets by
selecting it in one (Sales in 1993) and then making a group selection. Now you can confirm the formula as correct.

 Press Enter

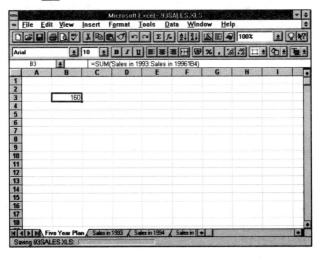

You could use the Fill handle to copy the formula to calculate the overall cash flow for the other quarters (by dragging to the right) or the other continents (by dragging down), but for practice do another one by hand!

🖰 *Repeat the process above, this time for B5, i.e. S. America's figures.*

Look at the formula in cell B4:

`=SUM('Sales in 1993:Sales in 1996'!B5)`

This formula, which refers to sheets specifically, is sometimes known as a **spear formula** because the formula 'spears' several sheets. A simple reference to a single cell on another sheet would take the form:

`=SheetName!Reference`

You can easily set up a link to cell on another sheet in this way. Suppose that you want to use some of the values from another sheet on this sheet.

🖰 *Select cell A3 in the Five Year Plan and type = While the formula bar is still active, click on the Sales in 1993 tab and select cell A4. Press* Enter

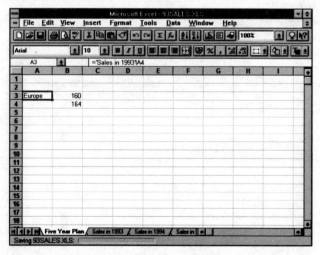

The formula =**'Sales in 1993'!A4** has been inserted into the sheet. This is by far the easiest way to set up links: simply click on the cell you need. It is important to realise that this is different from copying the data from one sheet to another: the contents of this cell will change as cell A4 on the sheet Sales in 1993 changes.

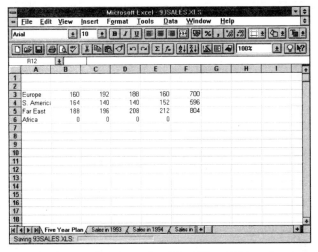

Complete the Five Year Plan to include all the data by using the Fill handle to copy the spear formula from B3 to new cells.

If you now look at cell F3 on the Five Year Plan sheet, you can see that the formula shows =SUM(**'Sales in 1993:Sales in 1996'!F4**)

Opening new windows on a workbook

Often, if you're working with several sheets, it is helpful to be able to see more than one worksheet at a time. Here, it would help to see two of the sheets from this workbook on the screen at the same time: the Five Year Plan sheet and one of the annual sheets. This can be achieved by opening up a new window, thus initially displaying the same sheet as the first window, but we can then change the sheet viewed in one of the windows.

🖰 *From the <u>W</u>indow menu, select the <u>N</u>ew Window option.*

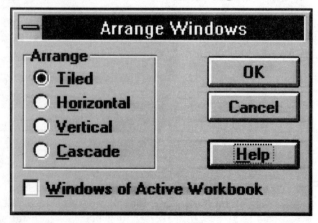

You still only see one window, but it is the new one. The :2 in the Title Bar indicates this.

🖰 *From the <u>W</u>indow menu, select <u>A</u>rrange...*

Arrange will arrange the windows by, for instance, dividing the display space equally between the two windows.

☞ *Choose* ● *Horizontal and check* ☒ *Windows of Active Workbook, to ensure that only the two windows of* 93SALES.XLS *are displayed.*

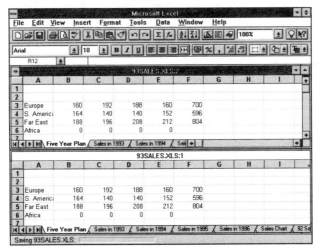

You can now see the Five Year Plan table in both windows.

Now we want to change one of them to display the annual sheet.

🖰 *Select the second window (93SALES.XLS:2) and click the Sales in 1994 worksheet tab.*

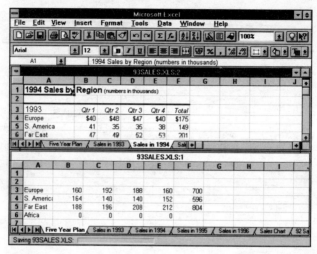

This gives a view of two separate sheets from the same workbook.

Copying across workbooks

Suppose you now want to take the Five Year Plan table and copy it to a new workbook which will contain similar tables from franchise sales regions around the globe. You can use the worksheet tab shortcut menu to do this.

First, you need to create the new workbook.

🖑 *Click*

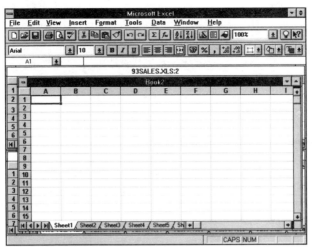

We want to see all our windows on the screen together, both the new workbook and the two windows for our sales company.

🖑 *Select Arrange... from the Window menu and choose ⊠ Tiled, checking that Window of Active Workbook is cleared.*

🖑 *Click*

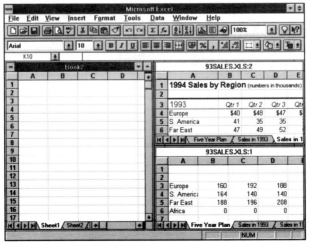

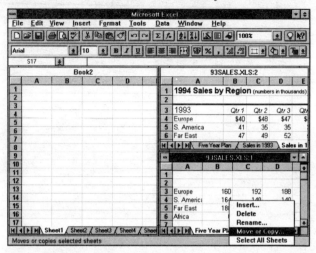

Click the Title Bar of the 93SALES.XLS:1 *window. Then right-click the Five Year Plan tab. (If it is not visible then scroll with the worksheet tabs until you can see it).*

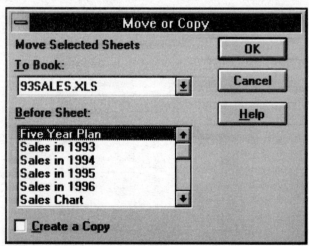

Select Move or Copy...

Currently, 93SALES.XLS is selected as the destination workbook. You need to change that to the new book.

🖰 *Click the drop-down button* ⯆ *for the destination work-book.*

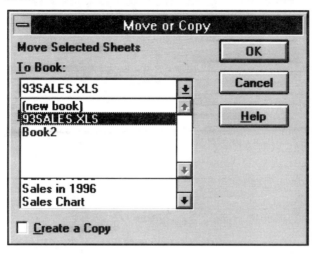

🖰 *Select the Workbook you just created (Book2 in the example here) and check* ⊠ *Create a Copy.*

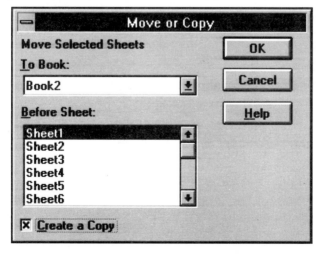

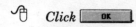

Click OK

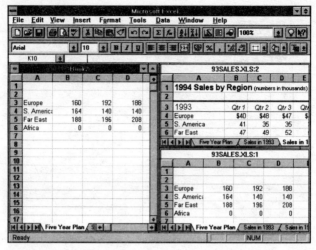

In anticipation of adding the other sales regions' data, save the new workbook and close it.

Save 93SALES.XLS *under a new name using File Save As... then select Close it. Also save and close the new workbook, calling it* FRANCHIS.XLS.

Summary: Manipulating the workbook

- You can use a worksheet tab's Shortcut menu for operations on the whole worksheet, such as renaming it, or copying the worksheet's contents.
- The Shift and Ctrl keys allow you to select several worksheets to work with as a group by clicking their tabs.
- You can have more than one window displayed for each worksheet.
- Window Arrange... offers options for displaying all open windows, or all windows of the active workbook only.
- Sheets can be copied between workbooks

15

LARGER DOCUMENTS

This chapter covers:

- Splitting and freezing windows.
- Zooming in on the worksheet.

——— Splitting and freezing ———

Large documents present special problems of their own. Therefore, there are special facilities to help you view, preview and print them.

✍ *Open the file* C:\EXCEL5\EXCELCBT\ACCOUNTS.XLS *and change to the Customers sheet by clicking on the correct tab.*

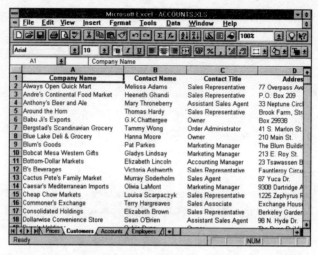

This sheet is not huge, but it is too big for one screen; so it is suitable for examining the principles of managing large spreadsheets.

Splitting the window

It is often convenient to be able to split the screen so that you can see your row and column headings whilst scrolling, or so you can see separate areas of the same worksheet. You can split a window horizontally or vertically by dragging either of the small black **split bars** ⊞ above and to the right of the respective scroll bars:

Position the mouse pointer over the vertical split bar so that the double-headed arrow pointer appears (⇌)

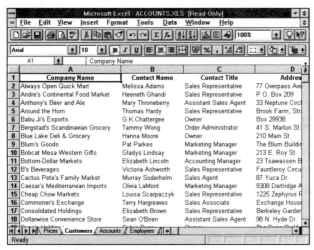

You could also use <u>W</u>indow <u>S</u>plit menu option to split the window.

Drag the vertical split bar down so that the split occurs directly under Row 1.

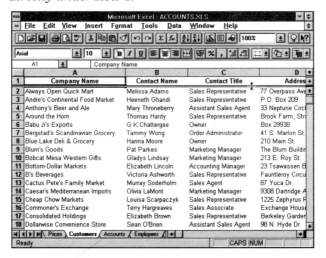

If you move the split bar while the cursor is over the scroll bar then completely free movement is possible, allowing you to position it anywhere; although if you move the split cursor when over the work-sheet cells, the split bar will travel to the nearest cell edge.

Notice that you now have two scroll bars on the right. The two **panes** can be scrolled independently. Thus, by scrolling the lower pane, you can leave the upper pane to provide headings or titles:

 Scroll down the lower pane.

In the following screenshot, you can see rows 1 and 86 are now adjacent, and that the bottom of the customer list is visible.

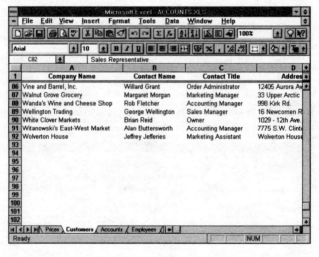

Scroll down the upper pane.

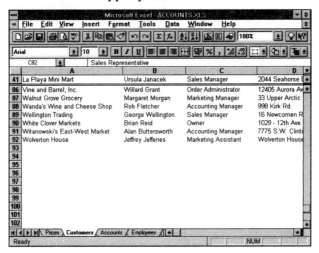

 Scroll back to the top of the upper pane.

Note that you can use ⌨F6 to jump the active cell between the panes. If you wish to remove the split at any time, you can drag the split bar back to the top of the appropriate scroll bar, or you could select Remove Split from the Window menu.

Freeze panes

Having split the screen and arranged to see those rows and columns you wish to see in a window, you could use the option Window Freeze Panes, so that certain information, such as titles, cannot be scrolled.

 From the Window menu select Freeze Panes.

Scroll down to see the Hugo Zajac details (line 29).

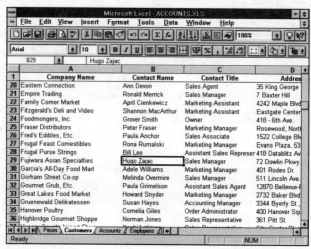

The top pane is 'frozen': the titles remain in place whilst scrolling down. There is only one scroll bar on the right now; there were two before, one for each pane. The single scroll bar refers to the lower pane. Only the upper pane is frozen and therefore cannot be scrolled.

It is also possible to use a simliar technique to split and freeze the worksheet vertically so that selected columns remain at the left of the screen while you scroll off to the right.

👍 *Often when you are freezing parts of the worksheet it helps to apply a light background colour to those cells so that it is clear which cells are frozen!*

Two-Dimensional Split

As well as splitting horizontally, it is possible to split the sheet in both directions simultaneously.

Use **W**indow Remove **S**plit to remove the currently split and frozen top pane.

For splitting in 2 directions at once you can use first one split bar, then the other, to create the desired split. Alternatively, you can pick an 'axis' cell and then use Window Split. The 'axis' cell should be the one which is directly underneath the last heading row and directly to the right of the last heading column. In this example, row 1 and column A are going to act as headings, and so we should split at cell B2 (immediately underneath row 1 and immediately to the right of column A).

🖰 *Select cell B2 and then take Split from the Window menu.*

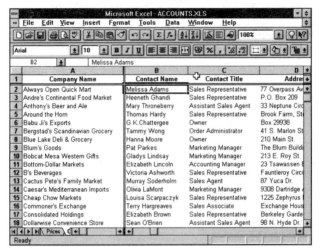

🖰 *Fix the headings in place using Window Freeze Panes.*

The row and column headings will now stay in position if you scroll off to the right, or off the bottom of the screen, or both.

🖰 *Remove the split by selecting Window Remove Split.*

--------------------- **Zoom** ---------------------

The zoom facility in Excel allows worksheets to be displayed on the screen at any scale from 10% to 400% of normal (i.e. the cells can be anything from one tenth to four times their normal size).

🖱 *Press* Ctrl Home *to return to the top left*

The Zoom Control drop-down is on the Standard toolbar
100% ⬧. You can either choose one of the preset zoom levels
in the drop-down, or type in a value of your own that is within
the accpted range.

🖱 *Click the Zoom Control drop-down button,* ⬧

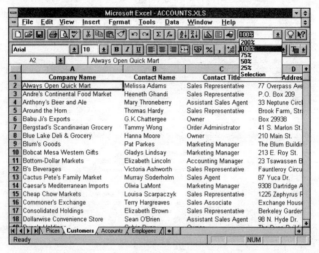

🖱 *Select a zoom level of 200%*

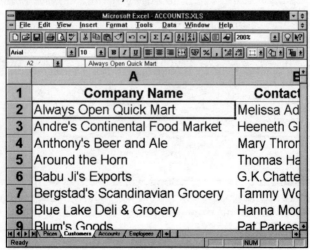

🖑 *Select a zoom level of 50%*

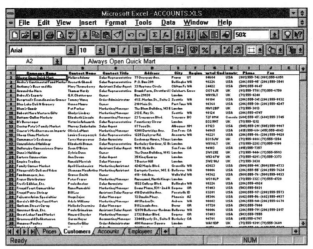

You can also zoom the display to fit a selection of cells.

🖑 *Select cells A1:G7.*

🖑 *Using the Zoom Control, choose Selection from the drop-down list.*

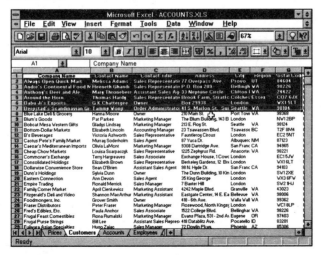

Excel zooms in as close as it can to display the entire selection (67%), but does not distort the display aspect ratio (that is, it does not stretch the display so that only the selection is seen), As a result, some extra cells are displayed under the selection.

 Zoom back to 100% view.

Summary: Larger documents

- Split can be used to divide a window into two editable sections horizontally and/or vertically.
- Freezing split panes allows you to keep titles on the screen while browsing associated data.
- Zooming lets you get a closer or more distant look at the worksheet display.

APPENDIX 1: KEYSTROKES

This appendix lists some useful keystrokes:

- `Ctrl` `A` means hold down `Ctrl` then press `A`
- Function keys are written as `F1` to `F10`

In this appendix, a large number of quick keystrokes are listed. For a complete list of keystrokes, refer in Excel help for 'keyboard shortcuts'.

Using the Clipboard	
`Ctrl` `X`	Cut the selection to the clipboard
`Ctrl` `C`	Copy the selection to the clipboard
`Ctrl` `V`	Paste contents of clipboard

Entering data

`F2`	Activates the cell and formula bar for editing
`=`	Begins a formula
`Enter`	Completes entering data
`Esc`	Cancels the current entry in the cell or formula bar
`Home`	Moves to the start of the line
`End`	Moves to the end of the line
`←Back`	Deletes the character to the left of the insertion point, or a selection
`Del`	Deletes the character to the right of the insertion point, or a selection
`Ctrl` `;`	Inserts the current date
`Ctrl` `A`	Displays step 2 of the Function Wizard
`Ctrl` `Shift` `A`	Inserts argument names and parentheses for a function

Working with workbooks

`Ctrl` `PgUp`	Moves to the previous sheet in the workbook
`Ctrl` `PgDn`	Moves to the next sheet in the workbook
`Ctrl` `F6`	Display the next window
`Ctrl` `Shift` `F6`	Display the previous window
`Ctrl` `7`	Shows or hides the Standard toolbar

Selecting blocks and Moving within them

`Shift`	With navigation keys, selects the cells you move across
`Ctrl` `A`	Selects the whole worksheet
`Enter`	Moves down through a selection
`Shift` `Enter`	Moves up through a selection
`Tab`	Moves right through a selection
`Shift` `Tab`	Moves left through a selection
`Ctrl` `*`	Selects the current region

Undo and Redo

`Ctrl` `Z`	Undo
`Ctrl` `Y`	Redo an action previously undone

Deleting, Inserting and Clearing

`Ctrl` `-`	Deletes the selected cells
`Ctrl` `Shift` `+`	Inserts as many blank cells as there are cells in the current selection
`Del` or `Ctrl` `Del`	Clears formulas from the current selection

Help

`F1`	Help
`Shift` `F1`	Activate Help pointer

EXCEL 5

Character formatting

Ctrl B	Make characters bold
Ctrl I	Italicise characters
Ctrl U	Underline characters
Ctrl Shift ~	Apply general number format

Moving in a worksheet

→	Move one cell to the right
←	Move one cell to the left
↑	Move up one cell
↓	Move down one cell
Ctrl →	Move to the right edge of the current block
Ctrl ←	Move to the left edge of the current block
Ctrl ↑	Move to the top edge of the current block
Ctrl ↓	Move to the bottom edge of the current block
PgUp	Move up one screen
PgDn	Move down one screen
Alt PgUp	Move right one screen
Alt PgDn	Move left one screen
Ctrl End	Move to the last cell of a worksheet (bottom right)
Ctrl Home	Move to the beginning of a worksheet

APPENDIX 2:
—— INSTALLING ——
EXCEL

This appendix covers:
- The system requirements for running Excel.
- The installation process.

—————— System requirements ——————

In order to be able to run Excel, your computer must meet certain minimum hardware and software requirements. Computers which do not reach these standards will not be powerful enough to run Excel 5, although you may find that they are able to run earlier versions of the package.

The minimum hardware your machine must have is as follows:

- An IBM PC or compatible, with an 80286, 80386, i486, Pentium or more powerful processor
- An EGA monitor, or some higher resolution (such as VGA) compatible with Microsoft Windows
- 4 MB of RAM
- A hard disk with at least 8 MB free (for a minimum installation of Excel only).

The minimum software requirements are:

- MS-DOS operating system version 3.1 or later
- Any of the following versions of Microsoft Windows:
  - Windows 3.1 or later in standard or enhanced mode
  - Windows for Workgroups 3.1 or later
  - Windows for Pen Computing
  - Windows NT 3.1 or later

──────── The installation process ────────

This section will consider the method of installing Excel on a normal, stand-alone computer. It is possible to set up Excel to run on a network, but that is beyond the scope of this book. You are referred to the Excel 5 manual that comes with the software for more information on that.

Installing Excel is a relatively simple process: the installation disks come with an automated installation program; all you have to do is make a few simple choices along the way. The installation process is conducted from within Windows. With Disk 1 of the set in drive A, it can be started:

- In File Manager, by double-clicking on SETUP.EXE
- In Program Manager or File Manager by choosing File Run, then typing A:\SETUP

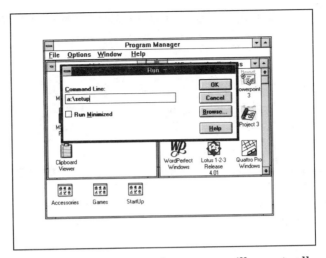

After checking your system, the screen will eventually show this:

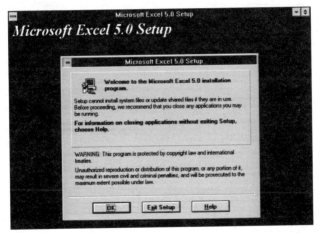

The setup program is now running. After other screens of information, (and which you get depends on whether you have installed Excel on your machine before,) you will arrive at the following screen:

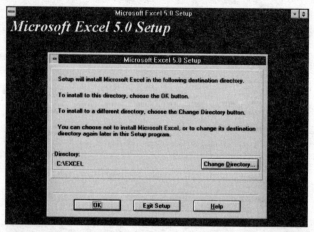

This is telling you where the setup program is going to put most of the Excel files. You should not need to change this, but it is possible to do so using the Change Directory button. Otherwise, use [OK] to proceed with the installation.

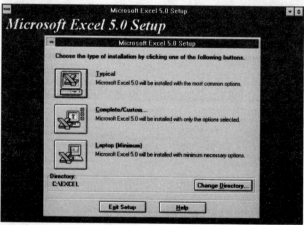

Excel offers you three different levels of installation: Typical, Complete/Custom, and Laptop (Minimum).

- Typical installation installs those parts of Excel used by the typical user. For everyday use of Excel, and for the things covered in this book, a typical installation would be sufficient. This form of installation will require 18 MB of free space on the hard disk of your computer.

- Complete/Custom allows you to pick which parts of Excel you install. If you need to limit the amount of space taken up by Excel, you may want to use this facility to pick exactly those features you require. A complete installation of Excel requires 24 MB of hard disk space.

- Laptop installation is a minimum installation – only those files deemed essential to Excel are installed on your machine. Since laptops usually have less hard disk space than other PCs, this minimum installation might be appropriate. A laptop installation requires 8 MB of hard disk space.

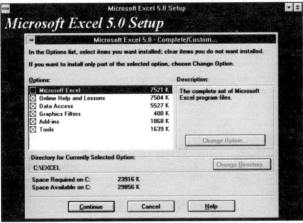

If you choose a Custom/Complete installation, the next screen will allow you to specify which parts of Excel you want to install. By clicking an option, you toggle between including it and excluding it. Towards the bottom of the dialog, there is a display of how much space the chosen installation will require, and how much is available.

After leaving this screen, you are asked in which Group in Program Manager you want the Excel icons to appear. Then, the installation process begins.

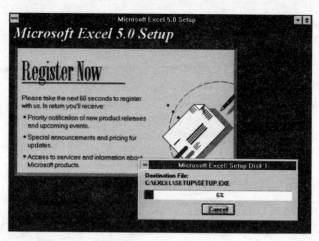

A dialog appears in the corner of the screen, showing how far through the installation process you are, and what file is currently being processed. Information screens will occasionally appear, telling you about Excel. One is shown here in the top left of the screen.

When all of the required files from this disk have been installed onto the hard disk, you will be prompted to insert the next disk in the series:

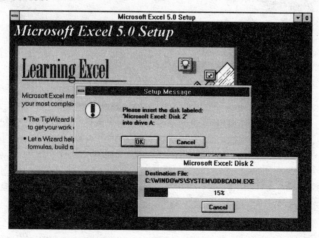

Replace the disk in Drive A with the next disk in the series, then click <u>OK</u>. Continue in this manner until you have completed the installation.

INDEX

ty TEACH YOURSELF

WORD 6

Teach Yourself computer books provide a full introduction to the major software packages available today.

Teach Yourself Word 6 is for first-time users of Microsoft Word for Windows version 6.

The book will give you a complete introduction to Word. It starts with basic word processing and shows you how to create professional-looking letters and documents. You will be shown how to edit text and how to handle documents, as well as how to undo mistakes, how to print your work and how to save it.

Once you can produce simple documents with confidence you can also learn how to use more complex features:

- changing the format of characters and paragraphs,
- creating bulleted and numbered lists,
- creating and manipulating tables,
- checking your spelling,
- creating and using styles.

About the authors
Oxford Computer Training are a leading computer training company. They are twice winners of Microsoft UK's Authorised Training Centre of the Year award for PC Applications.

Other related titles

TEACH YOURSELF

POWERPOINT 4

Teach Yourself computer books provide a full introduction to the major software packages available today.

Teach Yourself PowerPoint 4 is for first-time users of Microsoft PowerPoint for Windows version 4.

The book will give you a complete introduction to PowerPoint, enabling you to produce professional-looking presentations using your computer. It explains the basic principles, shows you how to make effective slides and acetates and how to run a slide show. You also learn how to edit or rearrange your slide show and how to save it.

Once you can produce simple slides with confidence you can also learn how to use more complex features:

- adding graphics to slides,
- using the ClipArt gallery,
- producing speaker notes,
- using PowerPoint with Excel 5 and Word 6,
- producing a fully automatic presentation.

About the authors
Oxford Computer Training are a leading computer training company. They are twice winners of Microsoft UK's Authorised Training Centre of the Year award for PC Applications.

Other related titles

WINDOWS™ 95

Teach Yourself computer books provide a full introduction to the major software packages available today.

Teach Yourself Windows™ 95 is for both first-time users of this operating system, and for those who are upgrading.

The book provides a basic introductuon to Windows™ 95. It covers topics from Desktop organisation, creating folders and using accessories through to printing, creating shortcuts and using the Briefcase and Explorer. There is also an introductory section on working with other users using the network neighbourhood.

Once you can tackle the basics of Windows™ 95 you can go on to use its more complex features:

- sharing data across applications,
- sharing files with other network users,
- setting up printers from your computer,
- using the Briefcase to control document versions.

About the authors
Oxford Computer Training are a leading computer training company. They are twice winners of Microsoft UK's Authorised Training Centre of the Year award for PC Applications.